TSO CLIST to TSO REXX:
Conversion Handbook

By Gabriel F. Gargiulo

Table of Contents

Table of Contents

Table of Contents

Table of Contents

Introduction

You have been given the job of converting a TSO CLIST to TSO REXX. You know how to program, and are familiar with the z/OS TSO/ISPF environment. You are not totally unfamiliar with these two programming languages.

CLIST is an interpreted language used in one environment: z/OS TSO/ISPF. There really is no other language like it, even if it bears a superficial resemblance to VM/CMS EXEC2 language and JCL procedure symbolic variables. CLIST is eminently suited for passing TSO commands to TSO, with or without symbolic substitution of values. In its infancy it had only rudimentary control structures, leading to programs that were difficult to understand and maintain. It has grown up, and now has respectable control structures such as subprocedures, DO WHILE and DO UNTIL.

REXX is an interpreted language used in several environments, such as:
- z/OS, (formerly called MVS and OS390) operating system
- JCL Batch jobs running under z/OS
- Netview for automated operations under z/OS
- z/OS TSO/ISPF Services for Panel Display
- QMF (Query Management Facility, a means for executing SQL)
- VM/CMS operating system
- CICS on-line system
- DOS/VSE operating system
- AIX
- AS400
- Linux

REXX has excellent control structures. It is possible to write a correctly structured program in REXX. REXX has an advantage over CLIST in the way it handles variables: it does not try to interpret data inside of variables, unless you tell REXX to do it. REXX has a large library of built-in functions that can simplify character string manipulation and interactions with the environment.

This book is about converting CLIST programs to REXX. It doesn't teach either language, as such, but you can use it as a reference for CLIST. This is not a cookbook. You need to know how to write programs, and need familiarity with the TSO environment.

This book will show you the features of CLIST and the corresponding REXX feature or nearest equivalent on facing pages. The CLIST language element will be on the left-hand page and the REXX language element on the facing right-hand page.

You will find examples of CLIST code and the corresponding REXX code on facing pages.

Introduction

I first encountered CLIST language in the mid 70's. My first reaction was a less-sanitized version of "What is this madness?" It was a set of CLIST programs that assisted in the day-to-day administration of TSO user-ids and authorizations. The programs became mine to maintain. I turned them into a complete set of procedures that automated the setting up of TSO user-ids and their authorizations. I also created CLIST code to audit the entire system to detect unauthorized changes. There was no REXX at the time.

I have taught classes to programmers on CLIST language (and REXX). Mastering REXX has not weakened my familiarity with CLIST language.

If you need more information about REXX, please refer to my book: *The REXX Language on TSO,* ISBN-10: 1479104779, ISBN-13: 978-1479104772, available for purchase at online booksellers and where you bought this book.

For the REXX functions see my book *The REXX Language on TSO: **REXX Functions**,* ISBN-10: 1490536078, ISBN-13: 978-1490536071, available for purchase at online booksellers and where you bought this book.

I've made the example code that goes with this book available. All CLIST code, and all REXX code that is named CLSTxxxx or REXXxxxx is available. You can find it here. Unnamed examples of code are not available.

The code is on the CBT tape, here: http://www.cbttape.org/cbtdowns.htmScroll down to File # 931.

REXX, TSO, ISPF, MVS, OS/390, VM/CMS, AS/400 z/OS, are registered trademarks of the IBM Corporation.

Gabe Gargiulo

Chapter 1: Discussion of Conversion

Chapter 1 discusses conversion from CLIST to REXX, and things to watch out for.

Chapter 1 contains:
        1.1 Warnings, Traps and Pitfalls

Chapter 1: Discussion of Conversion

1.1 Warnings, Traps and Pitfalls

Converting from CLIST to REXX is not a one-to-one conversion of language elements. It requires a knowledge of the environment in which CLIST and REXX execute, and the specific requirements of each language.

While both can do essentially the same thing, and you will always be able to duplicate the functionality, there may need to be some changes in the way the user runs the REXX program, as opposed to the CLIST. Also, error and abend handling are different, so the results will be different in case of difficulty.

There are many challenges in converting:
- CLIST programs can be very difficult to understand.
- The seemingly infinite nesting of variables can tax one's programming abilities.
- Several CLIST features just don't exist in REXX programs.
- Rudimentary control structures found in early programs will have to be converted to structured when they are placed in a REXX program.

Most elements can be converted without difficulty. The ones which will be a problem are:
- CLIST GLOBAL statement. There is no equivalent in REXX. ISPF variable services may be substituted, but it is not the same at all.
- CLIST NGLOBAL statement. This shares variables among all subprocedures and with the main part of the program in a CLIST. REXX variables in user-written functions/subroutines are shared with the entire REXX program, by default. There is no REXX equivalent to sharing variables among all subroutines.
- CLIST PROC statement. REXX does not work the same way at all. You can make it work in a manner that is close enough to the CLIST PROC statement to satisfy most users.
- CLIST GOTO. REXX SIGNAL is close, but not exactly the same. CLISTS that rely on the GOTO for major logic structures will have to be examined closely and be thoroughly understood before being converted.
- CLIST TERMIN. There is nothing like this at all in REXX. Besides, TERMIN does not work in ISPF, in the Session Manager or in a batch job.
- CLIST WRITENR. REXX has nothing that will display a string and leave the cursor at the end of the line for your reply.
- CLIST nested variables are something like REXX compound variables. Converting a program with multiple instances of variables within variables, sometimes to the second and third degree, can really tax your programming mind. It can be done, at the expense of clarity.
- Using the Line Mode Editor or other TSO commands that have subcommands will require you to put the subcommands in the REXX Internal Data Queue, or Stack. This is a straightforward conversion.

Chapter 2: The Basic Features of CLISTS

Chapter 2 presents a birds-eye view of the CLIST environment and the language. Please read this chapter in its entirety before proceeding. The corresponding REXX elements are shown on facing pages, to facilitate comparison.

Because there are so many critical terms used in this chapter, such as QSAM, panel, batch, I've defined and explained them all in Supplement 2, at the end of the book.

Chapter 2 contains:

Chapter 2: The Basic Features of CLISTs

2.1 What CLISTs are Used for

CLISTs are used to:
- Pass TSO commands to TSO
- Pass TSO subcommands to TSO commands
- Pass ISPF commands to ISPF.
- Perform calculations, character string manipulation and/or comparisons on data entered by the user at a TSO terminal.
- Display ISPF panels
- Execute ISPF panel commands that affect the display of panels
- Create ISPF EDITOR macros.

2.2 What CLISTs can do

- Perform arithmetic on numeric values
- Perform comparisons of numeric or character data
- Process nested variables: (a variable within a variable)
- Read, write or replace records in QSAM datasets ("flat files," or "sequential files") and PDS/PDSE members.
  It cannot process databases or VSAM datasets, or any other kind of datasets not mentioned here.
- Dialog with the user at the terminal, displaying messages and receiving replies.
- Establish a set of variables (GLOBAL) that are shared with CLISTs that your CLIST calls or is CALLed by.
- Pass commands to TSO, ISPF, and the ISPF EDITOR.
- Pass subcommands to TSO commands
- Submit JCL to the batch system for background processing
- Regain control in case of TSO command failure, or in case of an attention interrupt.

Chapter 2: The Basic Features of CLISTs

What REXX is Used for

CLIST and REXX are used for the same purposes. They do the same things, only differently.
REXX is used to:
- Pass TSO commands to TSO
- Pass TSO subcommands to TSO commands
- Pass ISPF commands to ISPF.
- Perform calculations, character string manipulation and/or comparisons on data entered by the user at a TSO terminal.
- Display ISPF panels
- Execute ISPF panel commands that affect the display of panels
- Create ISPF EDITOR macros.

What REXX can do

REXX does everything that CLIST does, except for the GLOBAL command and a few functions.
- Perform arithmetic on numeric values
- Do decimal arithmetic accurately, without losing significance in division.
- Perform comparisons of numeric or character data
- Process nested variables: (a variable within a variable)
- Execute data as REXX code: INTERPRET. REXX does it by choice. CLIST by default.
- Read, write or replace records in QSAM datasets ("flat files," or "sequential files") and PDS/PDSE members.
  It cannot process databases or VSAM datasets, or any other kind of datasets not mentioned here.
- Dialog with the user at the terminal, displaying messages and receiving replies.
- Pass commands to TSO, ISPF, and the ISPF EDITOR.
- Pass subcommands to TSO commands
- Submit JCL to the batch system for background processing
- Break apart character strings following specified criteria: PARSE
- Place data into a temporary area of memory for later use: the Data Queue (stack).
- Access a library of built-in functions for character manipulation, arithmetic and system information
- Allow the user to create reusable functions
- Regain control in case of TSO command failure, use of undefined variables, or in case of an attention interrupt.

Chapter 2: The Basic Features of CLISTs

2.3 How to Execute a CLIST

1. On any ISPF panel except option 6: (Setup required. See below)
```
   ==>    TSO Myclist or TSO %Myclist
```

> "%" before the program's name shortens search time for your program.
> It says: "it is a REXX exec or CLIST"

2. In the ISPF Editor: (Setup required. See below)
```
 EDIT        userid.TEST1.CLIST(Myclist) - 01.00
 Command ===> save;tso %Myclist      Scroll ===>
  ****** ********** Top of Data **************
 000001 WRITE THIS IS MY CLIST
 000002 WRITE EXECUTED ON &SYSDATE
```

3. On ISPF member list

        EX next to member name

```
 EDIT                userid.TEST1.CLIST
 Command ===>                                    Scroll ===>
           Name      Prompt      Size   Created   Changed
 _____    $I                   10   2021/10/18  2021/10/18 17:14:56
 EX_____   MYCLIST              15   2021/10/18  2021/10/18 18:36:28
```

4. ISPF option 6
```
                        ISPF Command Shell
  Enter TSO or Workstation commands below:

    ==>   Myclist or %Myclist (Setup required. See below)
    ==>   EXEC 'userid.TEST1.CLIST(Myclist)' /*(No setup req'd)*/
```

Chapter 2: The Basic Features of CLISTs

How to Execute a REXX Program
REXX and CLIST are essentially the same, except for the names and types of PDS's.

1. On any ISPF panel except option 6: (Setup required. See below).
       ==>   **TSO Tryrexx or TSO %Tryrexx**

> "%" before the program's name shortens search time for your program.
> It says: "it is a REXX exec or CLIST"

2. In the ISPF Editor: (Setup required. See below)

```
 EDIT           userid.TEST1.EXEC(Tryrexx) - 01.00
 Command ===> save;tso %Tryrexx          Scroll ===>
  ****** *********** Top of Data **************
 000001 /* REXX Tryrexx */
 000002 Say "This is my REXX program"
 000003 Say "Executed on" date(u)
```

3. On ISPF member list

       EX next to member name

```
EDIT               userid.TEST1.EXEC
Command ===>                                    Scroll ===>
          Name      Prompt      Size   Created   Changed
_____  $I                    10    2021/10/18  2021/10/18 17:14:56  RE
EX_____  TRYREXX               15    2021/10/18  2021/10/18 18:36:28  RE
```

4. ISPF option 6
```
                         ISPF Command Shell
  Enter TSO or Workstation commands below:
```

       ==>   **Tryrexx or %Tryrexx** (Setup required. See below).
       ==>   **EXEC 'userid.TEST1.EXEC(TRYREXX)' EXEC** /*(No setup req'd)*/

How to Execute a CLIST (Continued)

5. TSO in batch, with JCL. You can run a TSO session with JCL. (Beyond the scope of this book.)

6. Inside a REXX program
```
/* REXX  THIS WILL EXECUTE A CLIST 3 ways */
"Myclist"   /*(Setup required. See below)*/
"%Myclist"  /*(Setup required. See below)*/
"EXEC 'userid.TEST1.CLIST(Myclist)'"
```

7. Inside a CLIST
```
/* THIS WILL EXECUTE ANOTHER CLIST 3 ways
Myclist  /*(Setup required. See below)*/
%Myclist /*(Setup required. See below)*/
EXEC 'userid.TEST1.CLIST(Myclist)'
```

8. In native Mode TSO ("ready mode" or "line mode"). You type its member name.
```
   Myclist or %Myclist                   /*(Setup required. See below). */
   EXEC 'userid.TEST1.CLIST(Myclist)' /*(No setup req'd)*/
```

2.4 Setting up to execute a CLIST.

If you want to be able to execute a CLIST by simply typing in its member name in the PDS/PDSE in which it is found, you need to do some setting up.
One of the following must have been done:

1. Your installation has set up a JCL DD statement for the PDS/PDSE inside the JCL procedure which executes and starts up your TSO session when you log on. If this is the case, you need do nothing additional in order to execute your CLIST. You will be able to execute it by typing in its member name in the PDS/PDSE. Note that this is unlikely to be the case for development (testing) CLISTs.

2. During your TSO session, you connect the PDS/PDSE to the symbolic file name (DDNAME) SYSPROC by means of a TSO ALLOCATE command. The command is done as follows:
```
   ALLOCATE DDNAME(SYSPROC) SHR DSN('userid.TEST1.CLIST')
```

Note that this is not a good idea, if there is already an ALLOCATE command in effect which specifies SYSPROC. The PDS/PDSEs specified on the existing ALLOCATE command are needed, and you do not want to lose access to them. For this reason, many installations have devised a method to concatenate your CLIST PDS/PDSE to the PDS/PDSEs already specified on an existing ALLOCATE command. There may be a concatenate command that you can use.

3. Interactively, with an ALTLIB command.
If neither of the preceding two methods has been executed successfully in your TSO session, you can do an ALTLIB command. This tells TSO to look in the PDS/PDSE specified *before* looking in the PDS/PDSE(s) specified in any ALLOCATE DDNAME(SYSPROC) command
```
   ALTLIB ACTIVATE APPL(CLIST) DATASET('PDS/PDSE1')
```

How to Execute a REXX Program (Continued)
5. TSO in batch, with JCL.

6. Inside a REXX program
```
/* REXX THIS WILL EXECUTE ANOTHER REXX PROGRAM 3 ways */
"TRYREXX"    /*(Setup required. See below)*/
"%TRYREXX"   /*(Setup required. See below)*/
"EXEC 'userid.TEST1.EXEC(TRYREXX)' EXEC"
```

7. Inside a CLIST
```
/* THIS WILL EXECUTE A REXX PROGRAM   3 ways
TRYREXX  /*(Setup required. See below)*/
%TRYREXX /*(Setup required. See below)*/
EXEC 'userid.TEST1.EXEC(TRYREXX)' EXEC
```

8. In Native Mode TSO ("ready mode", or "line mode"). You type its member name.
```
   Tryrexx or %Tryrexx                         /*(Setup required. See below). */
   "EXEC 'userid.TEST1.EXEC(TRYREXX)' EXEC"        /*(No setup req'd)*/
```

Setting up to execute a REXX Program.
REXX and CLIST are essentially the same, except for the names of PDS's and DDNAMES.
If you want to be able to execute a REXX program by simply typing in its member name in the PDS/PDSE in which it is found, you need to do some setting up.
One of the following must have been done:

1. Your installation has set up a JCL DD statement for the PDS/PDSE inside of the JCL procedure which executes and starts up your TSO session when you log on. If this is the case, you need do nothing additional in order to execute your REXX program. You will be able to execute it by typing in its member name in the PDS/PDSE.
Note that this is unlikely to be the case for development (testing) REXX programs.

2. During your TSO session, you connect the PDS/PDSE to the symbolic file name (DDNAME) SYSEXEC by means of a TSO ALLOCATE command. The command is done as follows:
```
   ALLOCATE DDNAME(SYSEXEC) SHR DSN('userid.REXX.EXEC')
```

Note that this is not a good idea, if there is already an ALLOCATE command in effect which specifies SYSEXEC. The PDS/PDSEs specified on the existing ALLOCATE command are needed, and you do not want to lose access to them. For this reason, many installations have devised a method to concatenate your REXX PDS/PDSE to the PDS/PDSEs already specified on an existing ALLOCATE command. There may be a concatenate command that you can use.

3. Interactively, with an ALTLIB command.
If neither of the preceding two methods has been executed successfully in your TSO session, you can do an ALTLIB command. This tells TSO to look in the PDS/PDSE specified *before* looking in the PDS/PDSE(s) specified in any ALLOCATE DDNAME(SYSEXEC) command.
```
   ALTLIB ACTIVATE APPL(EXEC) DATASET('PDS/PDSE1')
```

Chapter 2: The Basic Features of CLISTs

2.5 Physical Characteristics of CLISTs

A CLIST can be a "flat file" (QSAM, sequential) or a member in a PDS/PDSE.
It is normally VB (Variable Blocked) with a record length of 255, and a block size of 3120. Your installation may choose other attributes. You should use those instead.
It may contain ISPF EDITOR line numbers, or not. I prefer not to use line numbers: (NONUM option of the ISPF EDITOR).

2.6 Passing Parameters to CLISTs

When you execute a CLIST you may pass one or more parameters to it. The CLIST will pick up the parameters on its PROC statement. CLIST supports positional parameters and keyword parameters.

```
%MYCLIST JOE DEPTA X4323 VACATION(YES)
EXEC 'userid.TEST1.CLIST(MYCLIST)' 'JOE DEPTA X4323 VACATION(YES)'
```

In this example, JOE, DEPTA and X4323 are positional parameters. The CLIST requires them, in this example, because it has a PROC statement specifying three positional parameters. VACATION is a keyword parameter. It is optional, by the nature of keyword parameters. The CLIST internally specifies the keyword parameter with or without a default value.

The positional parameters must be entered in the order established on the CLIST PROC statement. If one or more is missing, TSO will prompt you for them, in order. If a keyword parameter is not specified, the CLIST will use what is specified on its PROC statement.

If the CLIST is executed implicitly, as in the first line of the example above, simply by specifying its member name, then no apostrophes are required around the parameters.
If it is executed, as in the second line of the example above, with the EXEC command and the entire PDS/PDSE name, (explicit method) including member name, then apostrophes are required around the name of the PDS/PDSE, and also around the parameters.

Physical Characteristics of REXX Program files
This is the same as for CLISTs. Find out what your installation requires.

Passing Parameters to REXX Programs

When you execute a REXX program you may pass one or more parameters to it. The program will pick up the parameters on its ARG statement. REXX supports positional parameters. There are no keyword parameters.

```
%MYREXX JOE DEPTA X4323
EXEC 'userid.TEST1.EXEC(MYREXX)' 'JOE DEPTA X4323' EXEC
```

In this example, JOE, DEPTA and X4323 are positional parameters, or arguments, being passed to the REXX program. If the REXX program has an ARG statement, it will pick up the arguments. If you have an ARG statement and do not enter the arguments, nothing happens. There is no prompting for missing arguments. The variables are set to null.

If the REXX program is executed implicitly, as in the first line of the example above, simply by specifying its member name, then no apostrophes are required around the parameters.
If it is executed, as in the second line of the example above, with the EXEC command and the entire PDS/PDSE name, (explicit method) including member name, then apostrophes are required around the name of the PDS/PDSE as well as around the parameters. Also, you need the additional EXEC keyword at the end. This tells TSO that you are executing a REXX program.

2.7 CLIST Comments

The CLIST comment is delimited by /* at the beginning, and */ at the end. The */ at the end is not required if the comment is the last thing on the line of code, except for spaces.

```
SET MYNAME = JOHN /* FIRST NAME
SET MYNAME = JOHN /* FIRST NAME */
```

The CLIST comment is contained on one line only.

It may be between significant keywords of a CLIST instruction, in which case it does nothing. The WRITE statement just below displays: JOHN. The comment has had no effect.

```
SET MYNAME = /* FIRST NAME */ JOHN
WRITE &NAME
```

If it is found on a WRITE statement, the comment is displayed along with the other data on the WRITE statement. The WRITE statement just below displays: 09/09/21 /* TODAY'S DATE.*/

```
WRITE &SYSDATE /* TODAY'S DATE.*/
```

The comment may be before a CLIST instruction.

```
/* UNNECESSARY COMMENT*/ WRITE THIS WORKS
/* TRY THIS */ SET MYVAR = 1 + 1
WRITE &MYVAR
```

No problem if a comment is between keywords of a TSO command.

```
LISTDS   TEST1.CLIST /* DISPLAY INFO */ STATUS
```

No problem if it is before a TSO or CLIST COMMAND.

```
/* SHOW FILES */ LISTC
/* EXAMPLE OF SET */ SET VAR1 = HELLO
WRITE &VAR1
```

I never put comments inside of or before commands. I put them after commands, or on a separate line.
It is a good idea to create an initial comment at the beginning of your CLIST, but it is not required. If you do have one, please do not include the word REXX, or the REXX interpreter will be called.

REXX Comments
The REXX comment is delimited by /* at the beginning, and */ at the end.

```
MYNAME = "JOHN" /* FIRST NAME */
SAY MYNAME
```

The comment may carry over on to additional lines. Only the last line of the comment needs a */

It may be between significant keywords of a REXX instruction, in which case it does nothing. The SAY statement just below displays: JOHN. The comment has had no effect.

```
MYNAME = /* FIRST NAME */ "JOHN"
SAY MYNAME
```

A comment on a SAY does nothing.
```
SAY DATE(U) /* AMERICAN FORMAT FOR DATE */
```

The comment may be before a REXX instruction.

```
/* UNNECESSARY COMMENT*/ SAY "THIS WORKS"
/* TRY THIS */ MYVAR = 1 + 1
SAY MYVAR
```

No problem if a comment is between keywords of a TSO command.

```
"LISTDS   TEST1.CLIST /* DISPLAY INFO */ STATUS   "
```

No problem if it is before a TSO command, or before a REXX instruction.

```
/* SHOW FILES */ "LISTC"
```

```
/* EXAMPLE OF ASSIGNMENT */ VAR1 = "HELLO"
SAY VAR1
```

For REXX to work in all environments, regardless of the DDNAME allocations, you need a comment at the beginning of the program, before the first executable instruction, containing at least the word REXX.

```
/* REXX */
```

2.8 Continuation of Statements

When a line of CLIST code, or a TSO command doesn't fit all on one line, you may continue the statement. "-"as the last non-blank character on the line tells CLIST to join the line to the next line, and to keep any leading blanks on the second line.
"+" as the last non-blank character on the line tells CLIST to join the line to the next line, and to delete any leading blanks on the second line.

```
PROC 5 VAR1 VAR2 VAR3 +
    VAR4 VAR5


ALLOC DDN(ddname) NEW REUSE DSN('dataset-to-write')  +
  LRECL(record-length) RECFM(F B) SPACE(10 10) TRACKS


/* GIVES HELLO THERE  */
WRITE HELLO-
 THERE


/* GIVES HELLOTHERE  */
WRITE HELLO+
 THERE
```

Some control structures require a – or a + if they are on a line by themselves.
Labels for subprocedures and destinations of a GOTO instruction need a continuation, as shown in these examples:

```
MYSUBPROCEDURE: +
SET A = 1 + 2
RETURN



HERE: +
WRITE AFTER THE LABEL HERE
/* CODE */
```

THEN and ELSE require a continuation, if a DO follows.

```
IF &A = 123 THEN +
  DO
   WRITE IT IS TRUE
   /* CODE */
  END
ELSE +
  DO
   WRITE IT IS NOT TRUE
   /* CODE */
  END
```

Continuation of Statements in REXX

If your statement or TSO command doesn't fit on one line, you can continue it on the next line. A comma as the last non-blank character on the line tells REXX to join the line to the next line. A space is added between the end of the line, after the comma, and the next. If you want to join the two lines without any added spaces, use the concatenation operator: (||). On the mainframe this character is two of the solid vertical bars (hex 4F).

```
ARG VARIABLE1 VARIABLE2 VARIABLE3,
     VARIABLE4 VARIABLE5

"ALLOC DDN(ddname) NEW REUSE DSN('dataset-to-write')"  ,
  "LRECL(record-length) RECFM(F B) SPACE(10 10) TRACKS"

/* GIVES HELLO THERE  */
SAY "HELLO",
"THERE"

/* GIVES HELLOTHERE  */
SAY "HELLO"||,
"THERE"
```

A quoted string that is not closed at the end of the line is joined to the next line, with many additional intervening spaces.

You can use the concatenation character to eliminate the intervening spaces.

Logic structures don't need continuation in REXX.

2.9 The Semicolon to Delimit Statements

The semicolon is not used to join 2 or more TSO commands in a CLIST, or CLIST statements.

```
LISTCAT;LISTALC STATUS  /* DOES NOT WORK */
SET B = 456;SET C = 789 /* INVALID */
WRITE &B &C
```

2.10 Upper, Lower and Mixed Case in CLISTs

CLIST instructions and keywords must be in uppercase.

Variable names may be specified in upper or lowercase, and one is equivalent to the other.

All data that you enter is converted to uppercase, even if it is entered as lowercase or mixed.

To preserve case as entered, execute the CLIST statement CONTROL ASIS before the place where you need lower or mixed case.

TSO commands may be in upper, lower or mixed case. TSO converts them to uppercase.

```
WRITE ENTER YOUR NAME
READ NAME
WRITE THANK YOU &NAME    /* NAME CONVERTED TO UPPERCASE */
CONTROL ASIS
WRITE ENTER YOUR NAME
READ NAME
WRITE THANK YOU &NAME    /* NAME NOT CONVERTED TO UPPERCASE */
```

Data in a GETFILE or PUTFILE file IO statement is converted to uppercase, unless you have executed a CONTROL ASIS or NOCAPS statement before the GETFILE or PUTFILE.

The Semicolon to Delimit Statements (REXX)

You may put more than one TSO command or REXX statement on the same line. Just separate them with a semicolon.

```
"LISTCAT";"LISTALC STATUS"
B = 456; C=789
VAR1 = 0; VAR2 = 0; VAR3 = 0
```

No semicolon is needed at the end of each statement. However, it is not an error.

```
VAR1 = 0;
VAR2 = 0;
VAR3 = 0;
```

Upper, Lower and Mixed Case in REXX

REXX instructions and keywords may be in upper, lower or mixed case.

Variable names may be specified in upper or lowercase, and one is equivalent to the other.

All data that you enter is kept in the original case, unless you change it. The PARSE, ARG, PULL instructions, for example, will convert to uppercase if you add the keyword UPPER.

Data in file IO (EXECIO) is not automatically converted to uppercase.

TSO commands may be in upper, lower or mixed case. TSO converts them to uppercase.

Chapter 2: The Basic Features of CLISTs

2.11 Variables

The variable in a CLIST is a character string that begins with a letter or @#$_. The rest of the name may contain letters, numbers or @#$_.

You specify an ampersand (&) before the variable name when you are *retrieving* the value of the variable. The ampersand is not needed on a SET or on a statement that gives it a value.

Variable names should not be the same as CLIST statements, keywords, or TSO commands or subcommands. Even if you can prevent misinterpretation with a DATA – ENDDATA sequence, your program will be hard to understand.

See the chapter on subprocedures for information on how variables are shared in subprocedures.

If there is a GLOBAL statement in effect, some of your variables are being shared with CLISTs that execute yours, or that your CLIST executes.

To assign a value to a variable, you can use a PROC statement, a SET, a READ, or a GETFILE.

An undefined variable has a null value (zero characters.)

All variable names may end in an optional period (dot, full stop). The period is needed only when the variable is prefixed to another variable, a character string or another period.

```
SET LEVEL1 = PAYROLL
SET LEVEL2 = HOURLY
SET LEVEL3 = DATA
ALLOC DSN('&LEVEL1..&LEVEL2..&LEVEL3') SHR
```

This is true also for built-in functions and control variables:
```
SET DSN_TO_DELETE = '&SYSUID..ABC.DATA' /* REQUIRED PERIOD */
WRITE THE DSN IS: &DSN_TO_DELETE
```

```
SET NAME = JOE
WRITE &NAME. /* OPTIONAL PERIOD */
```

Setting variables.

To give a value to a variable you use the CLIST instructions SET, READ, GETFILE and PROC. Here are examples of SET. The variable name does not need to be prefixed with an ampersand, when it is being given a value.
```
SET VAR1 = ABC        /* SET VARIABLE TO A CHARACTER STRING */
WRITE &VAR1
SET VAR2 = &STR(ABC 123 12/22/21) /* &STR PREVENTS ARITHM. EVALUATION */
WRITE &VAR2
SET &VAR3 = ABC       /* THE & IS OPTIONAL ON THE VARIABLE BEING SET*/
WRITE &VAR3
SET VAR4 = &VAR3      /* SET VARIABLE TO ANOTHER VARIABLE */
WRITE &VAR4
SET VAR5 = &VAR3.A    /* SET VARIABLE TO ANOTHER VARIABLE, AND APPEND*/
                      /* THE PERIOD IS NEEDED */
WRITE &VAR5
```

Chapter 2: The Basic Features of CLISTs

Variables in REXX

The variable in REXX is a character string that begins with a letter or @#$_. The rest of the name may contain letters, numbers or @#$_.

A variable does not need any special character to indicate that it is a variable. Variables are resolved, unless they are in quotes or apostrophes.

Variable names can be, (but shouldn't be) the same as REXX instructions or keywords.

Variables are shared with subroutines and internal functions, by default.

Values are assigned to variables with an ARG statement, a PULL statement, the PARSE instruction, the assignment statement and by EXECIO.

```
NAME = "JOE" /* assignment statement */
```

An undefined REXX variable has a value equal to its name, uppercased.

A variable name never ends with a period. A period is used to construct compound variables.

Setting variables.

To give a value to a variable, you use the ARG statement, a PULL statement, the PARSE instruction, the assignment statement or EXECIO.

```
VAR1 = "ABC"
VAR3 = ABC 12/22/21          /* DIVISION WILL BE ATTEMPTED   */
                             /* GIVES 0.0363636363   */
VAR2 = "ABC 12/22/21"    /* quotes prevent division      */
VAR4 = VAR3              /* SET VARIABLE TO ANOTHER VARIABLE */
NAME.PHONE = "12345678"  /* compound var uses period     */
                         /* to delimit parts             */

SAY NAME.PHONE
```

Variables in variables.
Specify the lower level (inner) variable with two ampersands. The first ampersand is dropped, and the rest is placed in the destination variable, WHICHDAY in this example. The WRITE statement sees the variable &WHICHDAY, and then automatically sees that it contains another variable: &DAY. It resolves the value of &DAY and displays it.
TSO automatically resolves variables within variables, up to a default level of 16. You can change this by setting &SYSSCAN. (See the entry on &SYSSCAN in Chapter 3.)

```
/* CLST0001 TO ILLUSTRATE A VARIABLE WITHIN A VARIABLE */
SET DAY = MONDAY
SET WHICHDAY = &&DAY
WRITE THE DAY SPECIFIED IS &WHICHDAY /* GIVES MONDAY */
WRITE DAY IS &DAY
```

2.12 The Literal
You do not enclose literal data in quotes or apostrophes in a CLIST. If you need to prevent the CLIST from interpreting the data, you enclose the data in the &STR() function. (See also &STR in Chapter 3.)

```
/* CLST0002 TO ILLUSTRATE &STR */
SET NAME = JOE             /* NO LITERAL DELIMITERS NEEDED */

SET BAD_DATE = &SYSDATE /* WITHOUT &STR, DIVISION IS DONE */
WRITE &BAD_DATE           /* GIVES 0 */

SET GOOD_DATE = &STR(&SYSDATE) /* &STR NEEDED TO PREVENT DIVISION */
          /* TAKING PLACE DUE TO THE SLASHES RETURNED BY &SYSDATE */
WRITE &GOOD_DATE          /* GIVES DATE, CORRECTLY */


/* CLST0003 ILLUSTRATES HOW &STR KEEPS LEADING AND TRAILING BLANKS*/
SET NAME = &STR(     JOE)
WRITE XX&NAME.XX

SET NAME = &STR(JOE      )
WRITE XX&NAME.XX
```

Chapter 2: The Basic Features of CLISTs

Variables in variables in REXX

You can put a variable in another variable in REXX. Then you will have to use INTERPRET or the VALUE function to retrieve the hidden variable's value.

REXX does not automatically analyze a variable to see if it contains another variable.

If you nest variables at more than one level, you will need to do another INTERPRET or VALUE function.

Example showing the VALUE function:

```
/* REXX REXX0001 TO ILLUSTRATE VARIABLES IN VARIABLES */
DAY = "MONDAY"
WHICHDAY = "DAY"
SAY VALUE("WHICHDAY")     /* GIVES DAY */
SAY VALUE(WHICHDAY)       /* GIVES MONDAY */
```

The Literal in REXX

If you want something to be taken as a literal, you should enclose it in quotes or apostrophes. Then it will not be interpreted as a variable, or as an arithmetic operation.

If you specify a character string without a literal delimiter, REXX checks to see if it's a variable. If not, then the string is uppercased and taken as a literal.

```
/* REXX REXX0002 TO SHOW HOW IT HANDLES SLASHES IN DATA */
 NAME = "JOE" /* NORMAL WAY TO SPECIFY A LITERAL            */
 NAME = JOE   /* JOE IS UPPERCASED AND TAKEN AS A LITERAL.*/
 BAD_DATE  = 09/06/21   /* DIVISION IS ATTEMPTED = 0.1 */
 SAY BAD_DATE
 GOOD_DATE = "09/06/21" /* NO DIVISION IS DONE     */
 SAY GOOD_DATE

/* REXX REXX0003 LEADING AND TRAILING BLANKS IN LITERALS */
 NAME = "     JOE"
 SAY "XX"NAME"XX"


 NAME = "JOE      "
 SAY "XX"NAME"XX"
```

2.13 The Label

The label is the destination of a GOTO statement, or is the name of a subprocedure. It begins with a letter or @$_, contains letters, numbers or @$_, and ends with a colon. If it is on a line by itself, it needs a continuation character.

```
/* CLIST CLST0004 TO SHOW LABELS */
GOTO HERE
/* CODE */
/* CODE */

HERE: +
WRITE AFTER THE LABEL HERE
/* CODE */

GOTO THERE
/* CODE */
/* CODE */

THERE: WRITE AFTER THE LABEL THERE
/* CODE */

/* NO EXIT IS NEEDED BECAUSE CONTROL DOESN'T GO TO A SUBPROCEDURE */
/* EXCEPT THROUGH A SYSCALL */
MYSUBPROCEDURE: +
SET A = 1 + 2
RETURN
```

The Label (REXX)

There is not much difference between CLIST and REXX labels. REXX labels can be the target of a SIGNAL, a CALL, or a function invocation. No continuation character is needed after the label.

```
/* REXX PROGRAM REXX0004 TO SHOW LABELS */
SIGNAL HERE
/* CODE */
/* CODE */

HERE:
SAY "AFTER THE LABEL HERE"
/* CODE */

SIGNAL THERE
/* CODE */
/* CODE */

THERE:
SAY "AFTER THE LABEL THERE"

EXIT /* EXIT NEEDED SO CONTROL DOESN'T FALL INTO SUBROUTINE */

MYSUBROUTINE:
A = 1 + 2
RETURN
```

2.14 The Arithmetic Operators

CLIST math operations are adequate for creating, modifying and submitting JCL. But the result of division is always a whole number. $3 / 2 = 1$. You need to do an additional operation: remainder, to find out if the division came out right.

+	addition	
-	subtraction	
*	multiplication	
/	division (integer result only)	
//	remainder	(give the remainder of the division of two terms)
**	exponentiation	(negative exponents always give a result of 1. Fractional exponents don't work.)
()	for prioritizing the order of operations	

```
/* CLST0005 TO ILLUSTRATE CLIST ARITHMETIC */
SET TOTAL = 1 + 1          /* ADDITION */
WRITE &TOTAL               /* 2 */

SET TOTAL = 1 - 1          /* SUBTRACTION */
WRITE &TOTAL               /* 0 */

SET TOTAL = 16 / 4         /* DIVISION */
WRITE &TOTAL               /* 4 */

SET TOTAL = 16 / 5         /* DIVISION */
WRITE &TOTAL               /* 3 */

SET REMAINDER = 16 // 5    /* REMAINDER */
WRITE &REMAINDER           /* 1 */

SET TOTAL = 4 ** 2         /* EXPONENTIATION */
WRITE &TOTAL               /* 16 */

SET TOTAL = 4 ** -1        /* EXPONENTIATION */
WRITE &TOTAL               /* 1 */

/* DOESN'T WORK. FRACTIONAL EXPONENT   */
/* SET &TOTAL = 4 * 2.2 */   /* EXPONENTIATION */
```

The Arithmetic Operators in REXX

REXX does math using decimal numbers. Results are presented in decimal numbers. Significance is not lost in division: $3 / 2 = 1.5$.

+	addition	
-	subtraction	
*	multiplication	
/	division	
%	integer division (same as CLIST "/")	
//	remainder	(give the remainder of the division of two terms)
**	exponentiation	(negative exponents always give a result of 1. Fractional exponents don't work.)
()	for prioritizing the order of operations	

```
/* REXX0005 TO ILLUSTRATE REXX ARITHMETIC */

TOTAL = 1 + 1          /* ADDITION */
SAY TOTAL              /* 2 */


TOTAL = 1 - 1          /* SUBTRACTION */
SAY TOTAL              /* 0 */


TOTAL = 16 / 4         /* DIVISION */
SAY TOTAL              /* 4 */


TOTAL = 16 / 5         /* DIVISION */
SAY TOTAL              /* 3.2 */


REMAINDER = 16 // 5    /* REMAINDER */
SAY REMAINDER          /* 1 */


TOTAL = 4 ** 2         /* EXPONENTIATION */
SAY TOTAL              /* 16 */


/* DOESN'T WORK: FRACTIONAL EXPONENT */
/* TOTAL = 4 ** 2.2    /* EXPONENTIATION */
```

2.15 The Logical Operators

These are used with the conditional statements IF and SELECT. This information is repeated in the chapter on conditional statements. (Chapter 5).

=	or	EQ
¬=	or	NE	(¬ has the hex configuration of 5F on the mainframe.)
<	or	LT
>	or	GT
<=	or	LE
>=	or	GE
¬>	or	NG
¬<	or	NL

&&	or	AND
		or	OR	(| has the hex configuration of 4F on the mainframe.)

The Logical Operators in REXX

=   Equal. If numeric, when compared algebraically.
(1.0 is equal to 001.000.)
If not numeric, when padded with leading or trailing spaces.
("Sue" is equal to " Sue ".)
Case is significant: "SUE" is not equal to "sue".

<>   Not equal, the negation of "=".
Algebraic comparison and padding are performed.

><   Not equal, the negation of "=".
Algebraic comparison and padding are performed.

\=   Not equal, the negation of "=".
Algebraic comparison and padding are performed.

¬=   Not equal, the negation of "=". (¬ has the hex configuration of 5F)
(The symbol "¬" may not be found on all keyboards.)
Algebraic comparison and padding are performed.

^=   Not equal, the negation of "=".
(The symbol "^" may not be found on all keyboards.)
Algebraic comparison and padding are performed.

<   Less than. Algebraic comparison and padding are performed.

>   Greater than. Algebraic comparison and padding are performed.

<=   Less than or equal to. Algebraic comparison and padding are performed.

>=   Greater than or equal to. Algebraic comparison and padding are performed.

¬>   Not greater than. (The symbol "¬" may not be found on all keyboards.)
Algebraic comparison and padding are performed.

\>   Not greater than. Algebraic comparison and padding are performed.

¬<   Not less than. (The symbol "¬" may not be found on all keyboards.)
Algebraic comparison and padding are performed.

\<   Not less than. Algebraic comparison and padding are performed.

&   AND
| OR: either one, or both (| has the hex configuration of 4F on the mainframe.)
&&   Exclusive OR: one is true, not both.

2.16 Order of Evaluation of Statements

Prefix operators: + -
  Exponentiation **
Multiplication and division * / //
Addition and subtraction + -
  Comparison operations
  AND
  OR
  The order can always be determined through the use of parentheses. Terms in parentheses are resolved before terms that are outside of parentheses.

2.17 EXIT to End your Program

The CLIST instruction EXIT terminates your CLIST program wherever it is encountered. You may specify an integer on the EXIT instruction. That number is passed to the caller. If the caller is TSO, TSO sees the number as a return code from the CLIST. If the caller is another CLIST, the calling CLIST can see the number in the variables &LASTCC and &MAXCC. If the caller is a REXX program, the REXX program can see the number in the reserved variable RC.

If you want to exit from the current CLIST and from any calling CLIST, code EXIT QUIT.

However, if the CLIST calling yours has a CONTROL MAIN or a CONTROL NOFLUSH instruction in effect, control returns to that CLIST.

```
EXIT                   /* terminates the program */
EXIT CODE(12)          /* terminates the program, passing 12 to the caller*/
EXIT QUIT              /* terminates the program, and all calling CLISTs,*/
                       /* unless one has CONTROL MAIN or CONTROL NOFLUSH */
EXIT CODE(12) QUIT     /* terminates the program, and all calling CLISTs,*/
                       /* unless one has CONTROL MAIN or CONTROL NOFLUSH */
                       /* and passes 12 to the caller */
```

With CLIST, an END that is not being used for another purpose will end your program's execution. This is to be avoided.

Order of Evaluation of Statements in REXX

Prefix operators + -

Exponentiation **

Multiplication and division * / % //

Addition and subtraction + -

Concatenation: the blank space or spaces, the concatenation operator ||, abuttal, or placing two items next to each other with no intervening spaces.

Comparison operations

Logical and: &

Logical or: | &&

EXIT to End your Program in REXX

EXIT terminates your REXX program wherever it is encountered. You may specify an integer on the EXIT instruction. That number is passed to the caller. If the caller is TSO, TSO sees the number as a return code from the program. If the caller is CLIST, the calling CLIST can see the number in the variables &LASTCC and &MAXCC. If the caller is a REXX program, the REXX program can see the number in the reserved variable RC.

There is no equivalent to CLIST EXIT QUIT.

```
EXIT                   /* terminates the program */
EXIT 12                /* terminates the program, passing 12 to the caller*/
```

With REXX, an unmatched END is a syntax error.

Putting quotes around "END" causes it to be sent to TSO, the Line Mode Editor, or some other command processor that is available to REXX. REXX will not try to interpret it if it's in quotes.

This page intentionally left blank

Chapter 3: Control Variables and Functions

Chapter 3 is about functions, or executable subroutines, that are an integral part of the CLIST language. They allow you to perform character string manipulation, an arithmetic calculation, or to retrieve system-related information.

Chapter 3 contains:

3.1 Control Variables that Return Information about the Environment

They are presented with similar functions grouped together, and not in alphabetical order.

&SYSDATE Function

Returns current date in format mm/dd/yy, example: 06/09/21.

Slashes are interpreted as the mark of division, except in a WRITE statement.

Enclose the function in a &STR function to prevent division.

```
/* CLST0006 TO SHOW SYSDATE FUNCTION */
WRITE &SYSDATE
SET MYDATE =        &SYSDATE
WRITE &MYDATE       /* 0, BECAUSE DIVISION WAS DONE */
SET MYDATE = &STR(&SYSDATE)
WRITE &MYDATE
```

Modifiable: no.

&SYS4DATE Function

Returns current date in format mm/dd/yyyy, example: 06/09/2021.

```
WRITE &SYS4DATE

WRITE &SYS4DATE             /*  06/09/2021 */

SET MY4DATE = &STR(&SYS4DATE)
WRITE &MY4DATE              /*  06/09/2021 */
```

Modifiable: no.

&SYSDATE Equivalent in REXX

CLIST &SYSDATE and REXX DATE(U) will both return the date in the format mm/dd/yy, example: 06/09/21. REXX does not attempt division on the date.

```
/* REXX PROGRAM REXX0006 TO SHOW DATE FUNCTION*/
SAY DATE(U)     /* format 06/09/21  */
MYDATE = DATE(U)
SAY MYDATE
```

&SYS4DATE Equivalent in REXX

There is no exact equivalent in REXX; however, DATE(), with no parameters, gives you a date in this format: 06 Sep 2021

If you really need to produce the same result as CLIST SYS4DATE, you can use this code:

```
CENTURY = SUBSTR(DATE(S),1,4)
 DATE_NO_YEAR = SUBSTR(DATE(U),1,6)
 SYS4DATE = DATE_NO_YEAR""CENTURY
 SAY SYS4DATE   /*  06/09/2021 */
```

&SYSSDATE Function

Returns current date in a sortable format: yy/mm/dd, example: 21/06/09.

```
WRITE &SYSSDATE          /* 21/06/09 */
```
Slashes are interpreted as the mark of division, except in a WRITE statement.
Enclose the function in a &STR function to prevent division.

```
SET SORTABLEDATE = &STR(&SYSSDATE)
WRITE &SORTABLEDATE      /* 21/06/09  */
```

Modifiable: no.

&SYS4SDATE Function

Returns current date in a sortable format: yyyy/mm/dd, example: 2021/06/09.

```
WRITE &SYS4SDATE         /* 2021/06/09 */
```
Slashes are interpreted as the mark of division, except in a WRITE statement.
Enclose the function in a &STR function to prevent division.

```
SET DATE4SYEAR = &STR(&SYS4SDATE)
WRITE &DATE4SYEAR        /* 2021/06/09  */
```

Modifiable: no.

&SYSJDATE Function

Returns Julian date in format yy.ddd, where ddd is from 1 to 366, example: 21.160

```
WRITE &SYSJDATE      /* 21.160 */
```
Slashes are interpreted as the mark of division, except in a WRITE statement.

```
SET JULIANDATE = &STR(&SYSJDATE)
WRITE &JULIANDATE        /* 21.160 */
```

Modifiable: no.

&SYSSDATE Equivalent in REXX
DATE(O) produces the same result as CLIST &SYSSDATE.

```
SAY DATE(O)                 /* 21/06/09 */
```

&SYS4DATE Equivalent in REXX
DATE(S) produces almost the same result as CLIST &SYSSDATE. It lacks slashes, however. If you really need the slashes, the code just below will put them in the data for you.

```
SAY DATE(S)                        /* 20210609 */

TEMP_DATE  = DATE(S)               /* 20210609 */
TEMP_YEAR  = SUBSTR(TEMP_DATE,1,4)
TEMP_MONTH = SUBSTR(TEMP_DATE,5,2)
TEMP_DAY   = SUBSTR(TEMP_DATE,7,2)
SYS4SDATE_EQUIVALENT = TEMP_YEAR"/"TEMP_MONTH"/"TEMP_DAY
SAY SYS4SDATE_EQUIVALENT   /* 2021/06/09  */
```

&SYSJDATE Equivalent in REXX
DATE(J) produces almost the same result as CLIST &SYSJDATE. The period separator is missing, however. If you really need the period, the code just below will put it in the data for you.

```
SAY DATE(J)                        /* 21160 */

TEMP_DATE = DATE(J)                /* 21160 */
TEMP_YEAR = SUBSTR(TEMP_DATE,1,2)
TEMP_DAYS = SUBSTR(TEMP_DATE,3,3)
SYSJDATE = TEMP_YEAR"."TEMP_DAYS
SAY SYSJDATE                       /* 21.160 */
```

<u>&SYS4JDATE Function</u>

Returns Julian date in format yyyy.ddd, where ddd is from 1 to 366, example: 2021.160

```
WRITE &SYS4JDATE            /* 2021.160 */

SET JULIANDATE = &STR(&SYS4JDATE)
WRITE &JULIANDATE           /* 2021.160 */
```

Modifiable: no.

<u>&SYSTIME</u>

Returns current time in format hh:mm:ss, using the 24 hour clock, example: 14:15:22

```
WRITE &SYSTIME

SET THE_TIME = &SYSTIME
WRITE &THE_TIME             /* 14:15:22 */
```

Modifiable: no

<u>&SYSSTIME</u>

Returns current time in format hh:mm, using the 24 hour clock, example: 14:15

```
WRITE &SYSSTIME

SET SHORT_TIME = &SYSSTIME
WRITE &SHORT_TIME           /* 14:15 */
```

Modifiable: no

<u>&SYSTERMID</u>

Returns the ID of your terminal, for example:

```
WRITE &SYSTERMID

WRITE YOU ARE ON TERMINAL &SYSTERMID
```

Modifiable: no

&SYS4JDATE Equivalent in REXX

There is no exact equivalent in REXX. To produce a date in the format 2021.160, you can use this code:

```
TEMP_DATE = DATE(J)          /* 21160 */
TEMP_YEAR = SUBSTR(TEMP_DATE,1,2)
TEMP_DAYS = SUBSTR(TEMP_DATE,3,3)
TEMP_SYS4JDATE = TEMP_YEAR"."TEMP_DAYS

TEMP_SDATE = DATE(S)         /* 20210609 */
TEMP_CENTURY = SUBSTR(TEMP_SDATE,1,2)


SYS4JDATE = TEMP_CENTURY""TEMP_SYS4JDATE
SAY SYS4JDATE                /* 2021.160 */
```

&SYSTIME Equivalent in REXX

TIME() is the exact equivalent of CLIST &SYSTIME.

```
SAY TIME()                   /* 14:15:22 */

THE_TIME = TIME()
SAY THE_TIME                 /* 14:15:22 */
```

&SYSSTIME Equivalent in REXX

There is no exact equivalent for &SYSSTIME in REXX. To produce time in the format 14.15, you can use this code:

```
SHORT_TIME = SUBSTR(TIME(),1,5)
SAY SHORT_TIME               /* 14:15 */
```

&SYSTERMID Equivalent in REXX

SYSVAR("SYSTERMID") is equivalent.

```
SAY SYSVAR("SYSTERMID")

SAY YOU ARE ON TERMINAL SYSVAR("SYSTERMID")
```

&SYSLTERM
Returns the number of lines displayed vertically at your terminal, for example: 24.

```
WRITE &SYSLTERM
```

```
WRITE YOUR TERMINAL CAN DISPLAY &SYSLTERM LINES
```

Modifiable: no

&SYSWTERM
Returns the width in characters, displayed horizontally at your terminal, for example: 80.

```
WRITE &SYSWTERM
```

```
WRITE YOUR TERMINAL CAN DISPLAY &SYSWTERM CHARACTERS ACROSS
```

Modifiable: no

&SYSUID
Returns the TSO user-id with which you logged on during your current session.

```
WRITE &SYSUID
```

```
WRITE YOU LOGGED ON AS &SYSUID
```

Modifiable: no

&SYSPREF
Returns the character string that TSO is currently prefixing to dataset names specified without apostrophes (not fully qualified.) This defaults to your TSO user-id, unless your installation has decided otherwise. To change it, use the TSO command PROFILE PREFIX
It is not a good idea to change it from the default. Otherwise, dataset names specified without apostrophes and without a valid high level qualifier will be rejected by the system.
Note that the change persists through an exit from ISPF, and a logoff/logon.

```
WRITE &SYSPREF
WRITE THE DATASET PREFIX IS CURRENTLY &SYSPREF
PROFILE PREFIX(ABC)
WRITE THE DATASET PREFIX IS CURRENTLY &SYSPREF
PROFILE PREFIX(your-user-id)
```

Modifiable: no

&SYSLTERM Equivalent in REXX

SYSVAR("SYSLTERM") is equivalent.

```
SAY SYSVAR("SYSLTERM")

SAY YOUR TERMINAL CAN DISPLAY SYSVAR("SYSLTERM") LINES
```

&SYSWTERM Equivalent in REXX

SYSVAR("SYSWTERM") is equivalent.

```
SAY SYSVAR("SYSWTERM")

SAY "YOUR TERMINAL CAN DISPLAY" SYSVAR("SYSWTERM") "CHAR. ACROSS"
```

&SYSUID Equivalent in REXX

There are two equivalents in REXX: USERID() and SYSVAR("SYSUID").

```
SAY USERID()

SAY "YOU LOGGED ON AS" SYSVAR("SYSUID")
```

&SYSPREF Equivalent in REXX

SYSVAR("SYSPREF") is the exact equivalent in REXX.

```
SAY "THE DATASET PREFIX IS CURRENTLY" SYSVAR("SYSPREF")
"PROFILE PREFIX(ABC)"
SAY "THE DATASET PREFIX IS CURRENTLY" SYSVAR("SYSPREF")
"PROFILE PREFIX(your-user-id)"    /* SET IT BACK TO YOUR USER-ID */
```

&SYSPROC
Returns the name of the TSO logon procedure with which you logged on during your current session. A logon procedure is a set of JCL that is executed by the operating system, which starts your TSO session, and which defines datasets and PDS/PDSEs that your session will use.

```
WRITE &SYSPROC
```

```
WRITE YOUR LOGON PROCEDURE IS &SYSPROC
```

Modifiable: no

&SYSCLONE
Returns the name of the MVS system that you are currently on.

```
WRITE &SYSCLONE
```

```
WRITE YOUR MVS SYSTEM NAME IS &SYSCLONE
```

Modifiable: no

&SYSCPU
Returns the number of seconds of CPU time that your session has used. It is in the format SS.HH where HH = hundredths of seconds.

```
WRITE &SYSCPU
```

```
WRITE YOU HAVE USED &SYSCPU CPU SECONDS
```

Modifiable: no

&SYSSRV
Returns the number of SRM service units that your session has used.

```
WRITE &SYSSRV
```

```
WRITE YOU HAVE USED &SYSSRV SERVICE UNITS
```

Modifiable: no

&SYSPROC Equivalent in REXX
SYSVAR("SYSPROC") is equivalent.

```
SAY SYSVAR("SYSPROC")

SAY "YOUR LOGON PROCEDURE IS" SYSVAR("SYSPROC")
```

&SYSCLONE Equivalent in REXX
MVSVAR("SYSCLONE") is equivalent.

```
SAY MVSVAR("SYSCLONE")

SAY YOUR MVS SYSTEM NAME IS MVSVAR("SYSCLONE")
```

&SYSCPU Equivalent in REXX
SYSVAR("SYSCPU") is equivalent.

```
SAY SYSVAR("SYSCPU")

SAY "YOU HAVE USED" SYSVAR("SYSCPU") "CPU SECONDS "
```

&SYSSRV Equivalent in REXX
SYSVAR("SYSSRV") is equivalent.

```
SAY SYSVAR("SYSSRV")

SAY "YOU HAVE USED" SYSVAR("SYSSRV") "SERVICE UNITS"
```

&SYSDFP

Returns the level of DFSMSFDFP on your system.

```
WRITE &SYSDFP
```

```
WRITE YOUR SYSTEM HAS &SYSDFP SMSDFP
```

Modifiable: no

&SYSHSM

Returns the level of the Hierarchical Storage Manager, if any, on your system.

```
WRITE &SYSHSM
```

```
WRITE YOUR HSM IS AT LEVEL &SYSHSM
```

Modifiable: no

&SYSISPF

Determines if ISPF is currently active in your session, I.E., are you executing in an ISPF session. If so, you can execute ISPF commands.

```
WRITE &SYSISPF
```
Returns:
```
ACTIVE
NOT ACTIVE
```

Modifiable: no

&SYSJES

Returns the version and release of JES on your system if it is active.
```
WRITE &SYSJES
```

Returns:
```
JES2 Z/OS 2.1
```
Possibly

```
INACTIVE
```
if JES is not active.

Modifiable: no

&SYSDFP Equivalent in REXX
MVSVAR("SYSDFP") is equivalent.

```
SAY MVSVAR("SYSDFP")
```

```
SAY "YOUR SYSTEM HAS" MVSVAR("SYSDFP")
```

&SYSHSM Equivalent in REXX
SYSVAR("SYSHSM") is equivalent.

```
SAY SYSVAR("SYSHSM")
```

```
SAY "YOUR HSM IS AT LEVEL" SYSVAR("SYSHSM")
```

&SYSISPF Equivalent in REXX
SYSVAR("SYSISPF") is equivalent.

```
SAY SYSVAR("SYSISPF")
```
Returns:
```
ACTIVE
NOT ACTIVE
```

&SYSJES Equivalent in REXX
SYSVAR("SYSJES") is equivalent.

```
SAY SYSVAR("SYSJES")
```
Returns:
JES2 z/OS 2.1   Possibly

INACTIVE   if JES is not active.

&SYSAPPCLU
Returns the MVS APPC Logical Unit name of the SNA-addressable unit for APPC.

WRITE &SYSAPPCLU

Modifiable: no

&SYSMVS
Returns the level of the BCP component of MVS.

WRITE &SYSMVS

Modifiable: no

&SYSNAME
Returns the level of the system that you are running on.

WRITE &SYSNAME
Returns:
S001   Possibly

Modifiable: no

&SYSNODE
Returns the name of the node that you are executing in. You need this name to do a TSO XMIT command.

WRITE &SYSNODE
Returns:
NODE001   Possibly

Modifiable: no

&SYSAPPCLU Equivalent in REXX

MVSVAR("SYSAPPCLU") seems to be the equivalent for this in REXX.

```
SAY MVSVAR("SYSAPPCLU")
```

&SYSMVS Equivalent in REXX

MVSVAR("SYSMVS") is equivalent.

```
SAY MVSVAR("SYSMVS")
```

&SYSNAME Equivalent in REXX

MVSVAR("SYSNAME") is equivalent.

```
SAY MVSVAR("SYSNAME")
```
Returns:
S001   Possibly

&SYSNODE Equivalent in REXX

SYSVAR("SYSNODE") is equivalent.

```
SAY SYSVAR("SYSNODE")
```
Returns:
NODE001   Possibly

&SYSOPSYS
Returns the z/OS name, version, release modification level and FMID of BCP.

`WRITE &SYSOPSYS`

Returns:

    xxxxx   Possibly

Modifiable: no

&SYSRACF
Returns the status of RACF on your system.

`WRITE &SYSRACF`

Returns:

    AVAILABLE
    NOT AVAILABLE
    NOT INSTALLED

Modifiable: no

&SYSPLEX
Returns your MVS sysplex name.

`WRITE &SYSPLEX`

Returns:

    PLEX1   Possibly

Modifiable: no

&SYSSECLAB
Returns the SECLABEL for your TSO session.

`WRITE &SYSSECLAB`

Modifiable: no

&SYSOPSYS Equivalent in REXX
MVSVAR("SYSOPSYS") is equivalent.

```
SAY MVSVAR("SYSOPSYS")
```
Returns:

xxxxx   Possibly

&SYSRACF Equivalent in REXX
SYSVAR("SYSRACF") is equivalent.

```
SAY SYSVAR("SYSRACF")
```
Returns:
```
AVAILABLE
NOT AVAILABLE
NOT INSTALLED
```

&SYSPLEX Equivalent in REXX
MVSVAR("SYSPLEX") is equivalent.

```
SAY MVSVAR("SYSPLEX")
```

Returns:
PLEX1   Possibly

&SYSSECLAB Equivalent in REXX
MVSVAR("SYSSECLAB") is equivalent.

```
SAY MVSVAR("SYSSECLAB")
```

&SYSSMS
Determines if SMS is available for your session.

```
WRITE &SYSSMS
```
Returns:
```
UNAVAILABLE
ACTIVE
INACTIVE
```

Modifiable: no

&SYSSMFID
Returns the name of the system on which SMF is active.

```
WRITE &SYSSMFID
```

Modifiable: no

&SYSSMFDEF
Returns the system symbol specified in SYS1.PARMLIB member IEASYMxx on the SYSDEF statement.

```
WRITE &SYSSMFDEF
```

Modifiable: no

&SYSSTSOE
Returns the level of TSOE that you are using.

```
WRITE &SYSTSOE
```
Returns:
```
4010        Possibly
```

Modifiable: no

&SYSSMS Equivalent in REXX
MVSVAR("SYSSMS") is equivalent.

```
SAY MVSVAR("SYSSMS")
```

Returns:
UNAVAILABLE
ACTIVE
INACTIVE

&SYSSMFID Equivalent in REXX
MVSVAR("SYSSMFID") is equivalent.

```
SAY MVSVAR("SYSSMFID")
```

&SYSSMFDEF Equivalent in REXX
I don't know of any equivalent for &SYSSMFDEF.

&SYSTSOE Equivalent in REXX
SYSVAR("SYSTSOE") is equivalent.

```
SAY SYSVAR("SYSTSOE")
```

Returns:
4010   Possibly

Chapter 3: Control Variables and Functions

3.2 Control Variables that Return Information about your CLIST program

&SYSENV

Tells you if you are executing in the foreground, online, or in the background, in a submitted job.

```
WRITE &SYSENV
```
Returns:
> **FORE**
> **BACK**

Modifiable: no

&SYSSCAN

Tells you the number of times that symbolic substitution will be done on a variable in your CLIST that is currently running.

```
WRITE &SYSSCAN
```
Returns:
> **16**   (The default.)
> **0**   (No substitution will be done. A variable, with an ampersand, will be taken literally.)
> **xx**   (some other number that you have set.)

Modifiable: yes. Changes the setting for the duration of the CLIST, or until changed.
```
SET SYSSCAN = 0 /* Do not do substitution */
SET SYSSCAN = 2 /* Just do it two times */
```

&SYSICMD

Tells you the name by which the current CLIST was invoked, if it was invoked implicitly, by entering its member name on the command line.

```
WRITE &SYSICMD
```
Returns:
> member name of program in its PDS/PDSE.

Modifiable: no

&SYSENV Equivalent in REXX
SYSVAR("SYSENV") is equivalent.

```
SAY SYSVAR("SYSENV")
```
Returns:
```
FORE
BACK
```

There is no REXX equivalent for &SYSSCAN

&SYSICMD Equivalent in REXX
SYSVAR("SYSICMD") is equivalent.

```
SAY SYSVAR("SYSICMD")
```

Returns:
member name of program in its PDS/PDSE.

&SYSPCMD

Tells you the most recent TSO command executed by the CLIST. If none, then EXEC.

```
WRITE &SYSPCMD
```
Returns:
```
     ALLOCATE /* possibly */
```

Modifiable: no

&SYSSCMD

Tells you most recent subcommand of a TSO command executed by the CLIST

```
WRITE &SYSSCMD
```
Returns:
```
     FIND /* possibly */
```

Modifiable: no

&SYSNEST

Tells you if this CLIST was executed by another CLIST or not.

```
WRITE &SYSNEST
```
Returns:
```
     YES /* another CLIST executed this one  */
     NO  /* no other CLIST executed this one */
```

Modifiable: no

&SYSPCMD Equivalent in REXX
SYSVAR("SYSPCMD") is equivalent.

```
SAY SYSVAR("SYSPCMD")
```

Returns:
```
ALLOCATE /* possibly */
```

&SYSSCMD Equivalent in REXX
SYSVAR("SYSSCMD") is equivalent.

```
SAY SYSVAR("SYSSCMD")
```

Returns:
```
FIND /* possibly */
```

&SYSNEST Equivalent in REXX
SYSVAR("SYSNEST") is equivalent.

```
SAY SYSVAR("SYSNEST")
```
Returns:
```
YES /* another program executed this one  */
NO  /* no other program executed this one */
```

&SYSPROMPT
Tells you if TSO command prompting is allowed or not.

```
WRITE &SYSPROMPT
        ON          /* TSO is allowed to prompt for missing information*/
                    /* on a TSO command */
        OFF         /* prompting is not allowed. (The default) */
```

Modifiable: yes

```
SET SYSPROMPT = ON
LISTDS /* TSO will ask for the missing dataset name */

SET SYSPROMPT = OFF  /* (back to the default) */
LISTDS    /* TSO cannot ask for the missing dataset name*/
          /*  and the command will fail*/
```

This can also be set by the CLIST control statement CONTROL
```
CONTROL PROMPT /* same as SET SYSPROMPT = ON  */
LISTDS          /* TSO asks for the missing dataset name*/

CONTROL NOPROMPT /* same as SET SYSPROMPT = OFF */
LISTDS    /* TSO cannot ask for the missing dataset name*/
          /* and the command will fail*/
```

&SYSSYMLIST
Tells you if CLIST statements are displayed before symbolic substitution is done.

```
WRITE &SYSSYMLIST
```
Returns:
```
        ON   /* CLIST statements are displayed before*/
             /* symbolic substitution is done */
        OFF  /* CLIST statements are not displayed before*/
             /* symbolic substitution is done (the default) */
```

Modifiable: yes
```
SET SYSSYMLIST = ON        /* same as CLIST control statement */
                          /* CONTROL SYMLIST */
SET SYSSYMLIST = OFF       /* same as CLIST control statement */
                          /* CONTROL NOSYMLIST */
```

&SYSPROMPT Equivalent in REXX

The REXX PROMPT() function has the same functionality.

```
SAY PROMPT()
```
Returns:
```
ON          /* TSO is allowed to prompt for missing information*/
            /* on a TSO command */
OFF         /* prompting is not allowed. (The default) */


CLIST:      SET SYSPROMPT = ON         REXX: Call PROMPT "ON"
CLIST:      SET SYSPROMPT = OFF        REXX: Call PROMPT "OFF"
```

To change the prompt setting, you can also do the TSO commands
```
"PROFILE NOPROMPT"
"PROFILE PROMPT"
```

Some programmers use this style:
```
X = PROMPT(OFF)
```
Instead of
```
CALL PROMPT "OFF"
```

&SYSSYMLIST

There is no exact equivalent for &SYSSYMLIST in REXX. You can achieve the same functionality using TRACE.

```
SAY TRACE()       /* DISPLAYS CURRENT SETTING OF TRACE. NOT SAME  */
CALL TRACE "R"    /* DISPLAY RESULTS OF REXX INSTRUCTIONS         */
CALL TRACE "I"    /* DISPLAY INTERMEDIATE RESULTS OF INSTRUCTIONS */
CALL TRACE "OFF"  /* TURN OFF TRACING */
```

REXX TRACE has many more options that are not shown here, because there they work very differently from CLIST.

&SYSCONLIST

Tells you if CLIST statements are displayed after symbolic substitution is done.

```
WRITE &SYSCONLIST
```
Returns:
```
        ON    /* CLIST statements are displayed */
              /* after symbolic substitution */
        OFF   /* CLIST statements are not displayed */
              /* after symbolic substitution (the default) */
```

Modifiable: yes
```
SET SYSCONLIST = ON       /* same as CLIST control */
                          /* statement CONTROL CONLIST */
SET SYSCONLIST = OFF      /* same as CLIST control statement */
                          /* CONTROL NOCONLIST */
```

&SYSLIST

Tells you if TSO commands are displayed after symbolic substitution is done.

```
WRITE &SYSLIST
```
Returns:
```
        ON    /* TSO commands are displayed after substitution */
        OFF   /* TSO commands are not displayed after substitution */
              /*(the default) */
```

Modifiable: yes
```
SET SYSLIST = ON  /* same as CLIST control statement CONTROL LIST */
SET SYSLIST = OFF /* same as CLIST control statement CONTROL NOLIST */
```

&SYSASIS

Tells you if data that is entered is being converted to uppercase or not.

```
WRITE &SYSASIS
```
Returns:
```
        ON    /* data entered is not converted to uppercase.*/
              /* It remains as is */
        OFF   /* data entered is converted to uppercase. */
              /* (The default) */
```

Modifiable: yes
```
SET SYSASIS = ON  /* same as CLIST control statement CONTROL ASIS */
SET SYSASIS = OFF /* same as CLIST control statement CONTROL CAPS */
```

&SYSCONLIST

There is no exact equivalent for &SYSCONLIST in REXX. You can achieve the same functionality using TRACE.

```
SAY TRACE()      /* DISPLAYS CURRENT SETTING OF TRACE. NOT SAME  */
CALL TRACE "R"   /* DISPLAY RESULTS OF REXX INSTRUCTIONS        */
CALL TRACE "I"   /* DISPLAY INTERMEDIATE RESULTS OF INSTRUCTIONS */
CALL TRACE "OFF" /* TURN OFF TRACING */
```

REXX TRACE has many more options that are not shown here, because there they work very differently from CLIST.

&SYSLIST

CALL TRACE "C" is a close equivalent for &SYSLIST in REXX.

```
SAY TRACE()       /* DISPLAYS CURRENT SETTING OF TRACE. */
CALL TRACE "C"    /* DISPLAY RESULTS TSO COMMANDS */
CALL TRACE "OFF"  /* TURN OFF TRACING */
```

REXX TRACE has many more options that are not shown here, because there they work very differently from CLIST.

&SYSASIS

In REXX, TSO commands, subcommands, variable names, undefined variable names and REXX instructions are uppercased automatically, when being interpreted. You may specify them in upper, lower or mixed case. The contents of variables are not automatically uppercased.

These forms of PARSE will convert to uppercase:
```
ARG  /* DATA TYPED ON COMMAND LINE AT EXECUTION TIME */
PULL /* DATA TYPED IN RESPONSE TO A REQUEST FROM THE TERMINAL */
PARSE UPPER ARG  /* DATA TYPED ON THE COMMAND LINE */
PARSE UPPER PULL /* DATA TYPED IN RESPONSE TO A REQUEST*/
                 /* FROM THE TERMINAL */
```

These forms of PARSE will not convert to uppercase:
```
PARSE ARG  /* data typed on the command line at execution time */
PARSE PULL /* data typed in response to a request from the terminal */
```

To convert to uppercase: (A TRANSLATE with only one parameter, *string*, converts to upper case.)
```
NEW_STRING = TRANSLATE(string)
```

Also, to convert to uppercase:
```
NEW_STRING = UPPER(string)
```

&SYSMSG

Tells you if messages from TSO commands are displayed at the terminal, or not. It can be useful to turn off the message from a TSO FREE command that does not need to be executed, but it is not a good idea to hide messages from other TSO commands, such as ALLOCATE.

```
WRITE &SYSMSG
```
Returns:
```
        ON    /* messages from TSO commands will be displayed*/
              /* (the default) */
        OFF   /* messages from TSO commands will not be displayed */
```

Modifiable: yes
```
SET SYSMSG = ON   /* same as CLIST control statement CONTROL MSG */
SET SYSMSG = OFF /* same as CLIST control statement CONTROL NOMSG */
```

&SYSFLUSH

Tells you if the system can flush any nested CLISTs that are executing, when an error or interrupt occurs.

```
WRITE &SYSFLUSH
```
Returns:
```
        ON    /* the system can flush nested CLISTS */
              /* when an error occurs */
        OFF   /* the system cannot flush nested CLISTS when an error */
              /* occurs (the default) */
```

Modifiable: yes
```
SET SYSFLUSH = ON  /* same as CLIST control statement CONTROL FLUSH */
```
Note: If CONTROL MAIN has been executed, you may not set SYSFLUSH = ON
```
SET SYSFLUSH = OFF /* same as CLIST control statement CONTROL NOFLUSH */
```

&SYSMSG

All the functionality of &SYSMSG can be had by using REXX CALL MSG.

```
SAY MSG()
```
Returns:
```
ON    /* messages from TSO commands will be displayed*/
      /* (the default) */
OFF   /* messages from TSO commands will not be displayed */
```

```
CALL MSG "ON"   /* messages from TSO commands will be displayed*/
                /* (the default) */
CALL MSG "OFF" /* messages from TSO commands will not be displayed */
```

Some programmers use the style:
```
X = MSG(OFF)    or X = MSG("OFF")
```
instead of:
```
CALL MSG "OFF"
```

&SYSFLUSH

There is nothing at all like &SYSFLUSH with REXX. A REXX program that fails returns control to its caller. A few situations can kick you out of any and all REXX programs that are executing.

&SYSDLM

Gives you the position of the character string on a TERMIN statement that was entered by the user at the terminal during execution. (See the TERMIN statement in Chapter 10, Section 10.6.)

This is of no value in a CLIST executed in a batch job, or under ISPF, or the Session Manager since the TERMIN statement doesn't work in those environments. This leaves very few environments where this works.

```
    WRITE PLEASE ENTER A OR B
TERMIN A B /* user enters A */
WRITE &SYSDLM /* returns 1 */
```

Modifiable: no

&SYSDVAL

Gives you a null string, or the character string entered by the user in response to a READ without operands (See the READ statement, Chapter 10, Section 10.4.)

```
    WRITE PLEASE ENTER YOUR NAME
READ /* NO OPERANDS*/
WRITE &SYSDVAL /* RETURNS WHATEVER THE USER TYPED IN,*/
                /* WITHOUT CHANGE */
                    /* INCLUDING APOSTROPHES AROUND DATASET NAMES */
```

Modifiable: yes

Putting a string of data in &SYSDVAL allows you to use the READDVAL instruction to break up the data into several variables.

```
/* CLST0007 TO ILLUSTRATE &SYSDVAL AND READDVAL
SET SYSDVAL = A STRING OF DATA
READDVAL VAR1 VAR2 VAR3 VAR4 VAR5
WRITE &VAR1
WRITE &VAR2
WRITE &VAR3
WRITE &VAR4
WRITE &VAR5 /* IN THIS EXAMPLE, &VAR5 WILL BE NULL */
```

&SYSDLM
There is no equivalent at all for this in REXX.

&SYSDVAL
There really is no exact equivalent for this in REXX. If you are using CLIST &SYSDVAL to break up data into words, you can use REXX PARSE for that purpose.

```
/* REXX PROGRAM REXX0007 BREAKING UP DATA INTO WORDS. */
SIMULATE_SYSDVAL = "A STRING OF DATA"
PARSE UPPER VAR SIMULATE_SYSDVAL VAR1 VAR2 VAR3 VAR4 VAR5
/* IN THIS EXAMPLE, VAR5 WILL BE NULL */
SAY VAR1
SAY VAR2
SAY VAR3
SAY VAR4
SAY VAR5
```

&SYSOUTTRAP

Captures the displayed output of TSO commands, subcommands, other CLISTs, and REXX programs executed from within your CLIST. You set this to a value corresponding to the maximum number of lines of output that you want to capture. There is no practical limit. See SYSOUTLINExx and the accompanying example of code.

Modifiable: yes

```
SET SYSOUTTRAP = 0         /* Do not capture the output of commands.*/
                          /* (Default) */
SET SYSOUTTRAP = 100       /* Capture up to 100 lines of the output*/
                          /* of commands. */
```

&SYSOUTLINE

Returns a positive number indicating the number of lines of displayed output that a TSO command has displayed after you turned on &SYSOUTTRAP and executed a TSO command. See SYSOUTLINExx and the accompanying example of code below.

Modifiable: yes, but there is generally no reason to do so.

&SYSOUTLINExx

After you turn on &SYSOUTTRAP and execute a TSO command, a set of variables is created. The variables are named &SYSOUTLINExx, where xx is a positive integer corresponding to one line of the command's captured output. &SYSOUTLINE1 contains the first line of output, and &SYSOUTLINE9999 contains the 9,999[th] line of output, etc.

Modifiable: yes, if you wish.

See the example of code on the next left-hand page.

&SYSOUTTRAP, &SYSOUTLINE and &SYSOUTLINExx are used together to capture the output of TSO commands.

There are REXX equivalents for those CLIST statements.

```
CLIST: &SYSOUTTRAP = 100      REXX: CALL OUTTRAP "LINE.,100"

CLIST: &SYSOUTLINE            REXX: LINE.0

CLIST: &SYSOUTLINExx          REXX: LINE.xx (where xx is an integer).
```

With REXX, however, you do not have to use "LINE." as in the above example. You can use another variable name.

See the example of a REXX program on the next right-hand page.

Chapter 3: Control Variables and Functions

Example of code that goes with SYSOUTTRAP, SYSOUTLINE and SYSOUTLINExx.

```
/* CLST0008. THIS CLIST WILL EXECUTE THE TSO COMMAND LISTDS */
/* AND CAPTURE THE OUTPUT THAT IS NORMALLY DISPLAYED AT THE TERMINAL */
/* THIS EXAMPLE DISPLAYS THE CAPTURED DATA.      */
/* YOU CAN DO OTHER THINGS WITH THE CAPTURED DATA */
SET SYSOUTTRAP = 100              /* ARBITRARILY CHOOSING 100 LINES. */
                                  /* YOU CAN USE A DIFFERENT VALUE */
LISTDS   'userid.TEST1.CLIST'     /* USE A VALID DATASET NAME HERE */
SET SYSOUTTRAP = 0                /* TURN OFF CAPTURING. */
SET MAX_RETURNED = &SYSOUTLINE    /* HOW MANY LINES RETURNED */
SET INDEX= 0
DO WHILE &INDEX LE &MAX_RETURNED          /* NOTE 1 */
        SET INDEX = &INDEX + 1            /* INCREMENT INDEX */
        SET CURRENT_LINE = &STR(&&SYSOUTLINE&INDEX) /* NOTE 2 */
        WRITE LINE RETRIEVED IS &STR(&CURRENT_LINE)
                                                 /* NOTE 3 */
END /* END DO WHILE */
```

Note 1. Repeat as long as the index is less than or equal to the maximum number of lines that were captured by the SYSOUTTRAP.

Note 2. &INDEX is appended to &&SYSOUTLINE. &INDEX contains a number from 1 up, incremented by 1 each time the program goes through the DO WHILE loop.

&&SYSOUTLINE has two ampersands. When this instruction is executed, only one ampersand will remain. CURRENT_LINE will contain &SYSOUTLINE1 during the first iteration, 2 during the second iteration, etc.

Note 3. The variable &CURRENT_LINE is analyzed, and its contents are displayed. Its contents are the line of data corresponding to the number appended to &SYSOUTLINE.

```
/* CLST0009. THIS CLIST WILL EXECUTE THE TSO COMMAND LISTDS */
/* AND CAPTURE THE OUTPUT THAT IS NORMALLY DISPLAYED AT THE TERMINAL */
/* THIS EXAMPLE DISPLAYS THE CAPTURED DATA.      */
/* YOU CAN DO OTHER THINGS WITH THE CAPTURED DATA */
/* IN THIS EXAMPLE, THE DATASET DOES NOT EXIST    */
CONTROL NOFLUSH  /* NOTE 1 */   /* DON'T TERMINATE IF ERROR      */
SET SYSOUTTRAP = 100              /* ARBITRARILY CHOOSING 100 LINES.*/
                                  /* YOU CAN USE A DIFFERENT VALUE */
LISTDS   'userid.NOEXIST.CLIST'   /* DATASET DOES NOT EXIST       */
WRITE &LASTCC WAS RETURN CODE FROM LISTDS COMMAND /* NOTE 2 */
SET SYSOUTTRAP = 0                /* TURN OFF CAPTURING. */
SET MAX_RETURNED = &SYSOUTLINE    /* HOW MANY LINES RETURNED */
SET INDEX= 0
DO WHILE &INDEX LE &MAX_RETURNED
        SET INDEX = &INDEX + 1            /* INCREMENT INDEX */
        SET CURRENT_LINE = &STR(&&SYSOUTLINE&INDEX)
        WRITE LINE RETRIEVED IS &STR(&CURRENT_LINE)

END /* END DO WHILE */
```

Note 1. CONTROL NOFLUSH prevents TSO from kicking you out of the CLIST when a command or instruction fails.
We expect this one to fail.
Note 2. Displaying the last return code from a command or instruction. We expect it to be greater than zero, indicating a failure.

```
/* REXX PROGRAM REXX0008 WHICH WILL EXECUTE THE TSO COMMAND LISTDS
   AND CAPTURE THE OUTPUT THAT IS NORMALLY DISPLAYED AT THE TERMINAL
   THIS EXAMPLE DISPLAYS THE CAPTURED DATA.
   YOU CAN DO OTHER THINGS WITH THE CAPTURED DATA.
*/
CALL OUTTRAP "SYSOUTLINE.", "100"/* ARBITRARILY CHOOSING 100 LINES. */
                                 /* YOU CAN USE A DIFFERENT VALUE */

"LISTDS  'userid.TEST1.EXEC"        /* USE A VALID DATASET NAME HERE */
CALL OUTTRAP "OFF"
MAX_RETURNED = SYSOUTLINE.0
DO INDEX = 1 TO MAX_RETURNED       /* THIS LOOP DISPLAYS ALL LINES */
   SAY "LINE RETRIEVED IS" SYSOUTLINE.INDEX
END INDEX
```

Notes. You can use a different variable name other than SYSOUTLINE. With CLIST, you cannot.
The DO loop increments the variable Index.
If the dataset on the LISTDS command does not exist, the REXX program continues, while the CLIST on the opposite page is terminated. CLST0009 is an example of a CLIST that continues when the dataset does not exist.

&LASTCC

Outside of an ERROR routine, it gives the latest return code from a CLIST statement, TSO command, subcommand, other CLIST executed, or REXX program executed.

Every CLIST statement, TSO command, subcommand, other CLIST executed, or REXX program executed successfully outside of an ERROR routine sets &LASTCC to 0.

If you have an ERROR routine, control goes to the ERROR routine when there is an error. If you don't have an ERROR routine, the CLIST is terminated.

Inside of the ERROR routine &LASTCC has the return code for the error that sent control to the ERROR routine.

See the examples for &MAXCC below.

Modifiable: there is no reason to modify this. Allow TSO and the CLIST to set the value in it.

&MAXCC

&MAXCC works like &LASTCC, except that it contains the highest &LASTCC that has been returned, to date, in your currently running CLIST.

Modifiable: there is no reason to modify this. Allow TSO and the CLIST to set the value in it.

```
/* CLST0010 TO TEST &LASTCC AND &MAXCC */
ERROR DO
     WRITE &LASTCC    &MAXCC
     WRITE IN ERROR ROUTINE
     WRITE &LASTCC    &MAXCC
     RETURN /* IGNORE ERROR, GO BACK AFTER OFFENDING STATEMENT */
  END

  WRITE BEFORE DOING ANYTHING &LASTCC
  WRITE ABOUT TO EXECUTE BAD CLIST STATEMENT
  SET TOTAL = 1 + B
  WRITE AFTER BAD CLIST STATEMENT &LASTCC    &MAXCC

/* CLST0011 TO TEST &LASTCC AND &MAXCC */
CONTROL NOFLUSH /* TO PREVENT TERMINATION OF CLIST */
ERROR DO
     WRITE &LASTCC    &MAXCC
     WRITE IN ERROR ROUTINE
     WRITE &LASTCC    &MAXCC
     RETURN /* IGNORE ERROR, GO BACK AFTER OFFENDING STATEMENT */
END

WRITE DOING BAD TSO COMMAND
LISTDS TEST1.CLIST XXX /* BAD OPERAND */
WRITE AFTER LISTDS &LASTCC      &MAXCC
WRITE ENDING CLIST
```

&LASTCC REXX Equivalent

REXX RC is a close equivalent for &LASTCC. There is one difference. In REXX, RC is set only by TSO commands and subcommands. A non-zero RC does not automatically kick you out of the program.

```
"LISTCAT"
Say RC
```

&MAXCC REXX Equivalent

REXX has no equivalent for &MAXCC. If you want the highest RC to date, you have to implement some code that you execute after every TSO command.

```
MAXCC = 0
"LISTCAT"
IF RC > MAXCC THEN MAXCC = RC
```

Of course, you have to initialize MAXCC to zero at the beginning of the program.

This does not account for negative RC's! If you want to handle that situation, then you need a maxnegativecc and a maxpositivecc.

You might code something like this:

```
MAXNEGATIVECC = 0
MAXPOSITIVECC = 0
IF RC < 0 & RC < MAXNEGATIVECC THEN MAXNEGATIVECC = RC
IF RC > 0 & RC > MAXPOSITIVECC THEN MAXPOSITIVECC = RC
```

3.3 Built-in Functions
They are grouped together, and are not in alphabetical order.

&DATATYPE
Indicates whether a character string is numeric, double byte, character, or mixed.
Possible values are
      CHAR
      NUM
      DBCS
      MIXED (DBCS and CHAR or NUM)

```
/* CLST0012 TO TEST FUNCTION &DATATYPE */
WRITE  &DATATYPE(ABCD)  &STR(ABCD)                   /*CHAR*/
WRITE  &DATATYPE(1234)  &STR(1234)                   /*NUM*/
WRITE  &DATATYPE(1 + 1)  &STR(1 + 1)                 /*NUM*/
WRITE  &DATATYPE(10.20)  &STR(10.20)                 /*CHAR*/
WRITE  &DATATYPE(DSN.ABCD.DATA)  &STR(DSN.ABCD.DATA) /*CHAR*/
WRITE  &DATATYPE(ABCD1234)  &STR(ABCD1234)           /*CHAR*/
```

&EVAL
The WRITE statement and TSO commands don't do arithmetic evaluation of character strings. Use this on a WRITE statement or a TSO command to force arithmetic evaluation of character strings. Symbolic substitution is done on those even if you don't use &EVAL.

```
/* CLST0013 TO TEST THE &EVAL FUNCTION */
CONTROL LIST
 WRITE 1 + 1          /* 1 + 1 */
 WRITE &EVAL(1 + 1)   /* 2 */
 WRITE 1 + X          /* 1 + X */
 WRITE &EVAL(1 + X)   /* CLIST ERROR */

 ALLOCATE SPACE(&EVAL(1 + 1)) NEW DELETE
```

&DATATYPE REXX Equivalent

REXX DATATYPE is almost the same. There is a difference in how it analyzes a number with a decimal point. CLIST takes it as non-numeric, while REXX takes it as a valid number. See the following example of code.

```
/* REXX REXX0012 TO TEST DATATYPE FUNCTION */
SAY DATATYPE(ABCD) "ABCD"        /* CHAR */
SAY DATATYPE(1234) "1234"        /* NUM */
SAY DATATYPE(1 + 1) "1 + 1"      /* NUM */
SAY DATATYPE(10.20) "10.20"      /* NUM */
SAY DATATYPE(DSN.ABCD.DATA) "DSN.ABCD.DATA" /*CHAR*/
SAY DATATYPE(ABCD1234) "ABCD1234" /* CHAR */
```

&EVAL REXX equivalent

There is no REXX equivalent for &EVAL. If an arithmetic operation is in quotes, REXX will not see it and not perform it. If it is outside of quotes, REXX will perform it.

```
/* REXX0013 TO SHOW USE OF QUOTES */
TRACE C
SAY "1 + 1" /* 1 + 1 */
SAY 1 + 1   /* 2 */
SAY "1 + X" /* 1 + X */
SAY 1 + X   /* ERROR */

"ALLOCATE SPACE("1 + 1") NEW DELETE"
```

&LENGTH

Gives the length, in characters, of a character string, ignoring leading and trailing spaces.

```
/* CLST0014 TO TEST THE &LENGTH FUNCTION */
WRITE &LENGTH(ABCD)               /* 4 */
WRITE &LENGTH(1 + 2)             /* 1 */
SET &VAR = &STR(1 + 2)
WRITE &LENGTH(&VAR)               /* 1 WORKS THE SAME WITH A VARIABLE */
WRITE &LENGTH(&STR(1 + 2))       /* 5 */
WRITE &LENGTH(    ABCD)           /* 4 */
WRITE &LENGTH(&STR(    ABCD))     /* 8 */
WRITE &LENGTH(ABCD    )           /* 4 */
WRITE &LENGTH(&STR(ABCD    ))     /* 8 */
```

&SYSCLENGTH

Gives the length, in characters, of a DBCS character string.

&NRSTR

Keeps the first ampersand when there are two ampersands prefixing a variable.
Useful when you have a string that contains a JCL temporary dataset name, such as &&TEMP.

```
/* CLST0015 TO ILLUSTRATE THE &NRSTR FUNCTION */
SET X = &NRSTR(DSN=&&TEMP,DISP=(NEW,PASS))
WRITE &X     /* DSN=&TEMP,DISP=(NEW,PASS) */
```

&LENGTH Equivalent in REXX

The REXX equivalent is LENGTH(). Compare the output of &LENGTH and LENGTH(). They are the same, in the examples.

```
/* REXX REXX0014 TO TEST THE LENGTH FUNCTION */
SAY LENGTH(ABCD)           /* 4 */
SAY LENGTH(1 + 2)          /* 1 */
VAR = 1 + 2
SAY LENGTH(VAR)            /* 1 WORKS THE SAME WITH VARIABLE */
SAY LENGTH("1 + 2")        /* 5 */
SAY LENGTH(      ABCD)     /* 4 */
SAY LENGTH("     ABCD")    /* 8 */
SAY LENGTH(ABCD      )     /* 4 */
SAY LENGTH("ABCD     ")    /* 8 */
```

&SYSCLENGTH

Use the standard REXX function length to get the length of a DBCS character string.

&NRSTR

There is no REXX equivalent, because REXX does not process variables the same way as CLIST.

&SYSNSUB

WRITE &SYSNSUB(*levels,variable*)

This can be used to limit the number of times (*levels*) symbolic substitution is performed in a *variable*. A zero value prevents any symbolic substitution.

The maximum value is 99.

```
SET TEMPNAME = JOE
SET THE_DSN = &SYSNSUB(0,&TEMPNAME) /* SETS IT TO &TEMPNAME */
WRITE &THE_DSN  /* JOE */
```

Suppose you have nested variables. There are three levels in the following example. You want to limit symbolic substitution to two levels. You can use &SYSNSUB to set the limit to two levels, or any other level that you want.

```
/* CLST0016 TO ILLUSTRATE THE &SYSNSUB FUNCTION */
SET LEVEL1 = JOE
SET LEVEL2 =  &&LEVEL1 /* FIRST  LEVEL VARIABLE IS PUT IN &LEVEL2 */
SET LEVEL3 =  &&LEVEL2 /* SECOND LEVEL VARIABLE IS PUT IN &LEVEL3 */
WRITE &LEVEL3 /* GIVES "JOE" */
WRITE &SYSNSUB(0,&LEVEL3) /* GIVES "&LEVEL3" */
WRITE &SYSNSUB(1,&LEVEL3) /* GIVES "&LEVEL2" */
WRITE &SYSNSUB(2,&LEVEL3) /* GIVES "&LEVEL1" */
WRITE &SYSNSUB(3,&LEVEL3) /* GIVES "JOE"        */
```

&SYSNSUB
There is no REXX equivalent, because REXX does not process variables the same way as CLIST.

&STR
Means that CLIST should take as a literal, without arithmetic evaluation, the information between the parentheses.
Note: the WRITE statement and TSO commands don't do arithmetic evaluation, but do symbolic substitution.

```
/* CLST0017 TO ILLUSTRATE &STR FUNCTION */
SET MYVAR = &STR(1 + 2)    /* NO MATH DONE */
WRITE &MYVAR               /* 1 + 2 */
SET VAR1   = &MYVAR        /* THIS DOES THE MATH */
WRITE &VAR1                /* 3 */
SET VAR2   = &STR(&MYVAR)  /* DOESN'T DO MATH */
WRITE &VAR2                /* 1 + 2 */
```

&STR is often used around the results of &SYSDATE, since &SYSDATE returns a date with slashes, which CLIST will interpret as division.

```
/* CLST0018 TO ILLUSTRATE &STR WITH &SYSDATE
SET MYVAR = &SYSDATE
SET VAR1 = &MYVAR
WRITE &VAR1                    /* 0 BECAUSE IT DOES DIVISION ON DATA */
SET MYVAR = &STR(&SYSDATE)
SET VAR1 = &STR(&MYVAR)
WRITE &VAR1                    /* TODAY'S DATE */
```

Setting a variable to a parenthesis.
To set a variable to a right and a left parenthesis, do:
```
/* CLST0019 TO ILLUSTRATE SETTING TO PARENTHESIS */
SET &RPAREN = )
SET &LPAREN = &STR((
WRITE &RPAREN &LPAREN
```

Preventing misinterpretation of a TSO command with the same name as a CLIST instruction.
If your installation has written a program or a command with the same name as a CLIST command, enclose it in &STR to prevent CLIST from trying to interpret it.
Alternatively, putting the command in a variable will produce the same result.
```
/* CLST0020 TO ILLUSTRATE &STR AROUND THE NAME OF A COMMAND */
/* ASSUMING THAT YOUR INSTALLATION HAS A PROGRAM NAMED "SELECT" */
CONTROL LIST /* SO YOU SEE WHAT IT IS TRYING TO EXECUTE */

&STR(SELECT) /* EXECUTES THE PROGRAM SELECT, NOT THE CLIST COMMAND */

SET &TSOCOMMAND = &STR(SELECT) /* ALSO CAN PUT IT IN A VARIABLE */
&TSOCOMMAND
```

&STR Equivalent in REXX
&STR in CLIST and quotes or apostrophes in REXX both cause a character string to be taken literally, without any arithmetic or variable resolution.

```
/* REXX0017 TO ILLUSTRATE LITERALS AND MATH OPERATIONS */
MYVAR = "1 + 2"                    /* NO MATH DONE */
SAY MYVAR                          /* 1 + 2 */
VAR1 = MYVAR                       /* THIS DOES THE MATH */
SAY VAR1                           /* 3 */
/* NO REXX EQUIVALENT OF CLIST SET VAR2   = &STR(&MYVAR) */


/* REXX REXX0018 TO ILLUSTRATE DATE FUNCTION */
MYVAR = DATE(U)    /* USA FORMAT FOR DATE */
VAR1  = MYVAR      /* DOES NOT DO MATH ON DATA IN A VARIABLE */
SAY VAR1           /* TODAY'S DATE */
```

Setting a variable to a parenthesis in REXX.
REXX doesn't get confused by parentheses like CLIST does. If the parenthesis is part of an instruction or function, it is not put in quotes. If you don't want REXX to see the parentheses, and not try to interpret it, enclose it in quotes as you would any other literal string.
```
/* REXX REXX0019 SETTING A VARIABLE TO PARENTHESIS*/
RPAREN = ")"
LPAREN = "("
SAY RPAREN LPAREN
```

The parentheses are in quotes in the following example:
```
"ALLOCATE DDNAME(INFILE)  SHR REUSE DSN('userid.TEST.DATA')"
```

Preventing misinterpretation of a TSO command with the same name as a REXX instruction.
```
/* REXX REXX0020 TO ILLUSTRATE RUNNING A TSO COMMAND
   THAT HAS THE SAME NAME AS A REXX KEYWORD (NOT A GOOD PRACTICE)
   ASSUMING THAT YOUR INSTALLATION HAS A PROGRAM NAMED SELECT
*/
"SELECT" /* EXECUTES THE PROGRAM SELECT, NOT THE REXX KEYWORD */

 TSOCOMMAND = "SELECT" /* ALSO CAN PUT IT IN A VARIABLE */
 TSOCOMMAND

"" SELECT /* THIS WORKS TOO, BUT IS STRANGE */
```

&SUBSTR

SET new_var = &SUBSTR(*startpos*:*endpos*,*string*)

Returns a part of a character *string*, beginning at *startpos* and ending at *endpos*. If you omit *endpos*, it defaults to *startpos*.

```
/* CLST0021 TO ILLUSTRATE &SUBSTR FUNCTION */
WRITE &SUBSTR(1:2,ABCD)        /* GIVES "AB" */
WRITE &SUBSTR(3:3,1+2+3+4)     /* DOESN'T DO MATH ON THE STRING.
                               /* RETURNS "2" */
```

&SYSCSUBSTR

SET new_var = &SUBSTR(*startpos*:*endpos*,*string*)

Returns a part of a DBCS character *string*, beginning at *startpos* and ending at *endpos*. The characters in the DBCS string are treated as individual characters.

```
WRITE &SYSCSUBSTR(2:3,<D1F2D3>) /* GIVES "D1" */
```
See Supplement 4.

&SYSCAPS

This is used to convert a character string to uppercase. This means that a previous CONTROL ASIS or CONTROL NOCAPS or SET SYSCAPS = OFF was done, otherwise everything would already be in caps.

```
WRITE &SYSCAPS(lowercase data) /* converts to uppercase */
```

```
/* CLST0022 TO ILLUSTRATE &SYSCAPS */
CONTROL ASIS
WRITE PLEASE ENTER YOUR NAME
READ NAME
WRITE THANK YOU, &NAME            /* DISPLAYS THE NAME AS ENTERED */
WRITE THANK YOU, &SYSCAPS(&NAME) /* DISPLAYS UPPERCASED NAME */
```

&SUBSTR Equivalent in REXX

SUBSTR() works the same way as &SUBSTR. The syntax is slightly different, however.
NEW_VAR = SUBSTR(*string, start-position, length*)

```
/* REXX PROGRAM REXX0021 TO ILLUSTRATE SUBSTR FUNCTION */
SAY SUBSTR("ABCD",1,2)         /* GIVES "AB" */
SAY SUBSTR(1+2+3+4,3,1)        /* DOES  MATH ON THE STRING. */
                              /* RETURNS SPACE */
SAY SUBSTR("1+2+3+4",3,1)      /* DOESN'T DO MATH ON THE STRING.*/
                              /* RETURNS "2" */
```

&SYSCSUBSTR

Use the standard REXX SUBSTR function.

&SYSCAPS Equivalent in REXX

In REXX, TSO commands, subcommands, variable names, undefined variable names and REXX instructions are uppercased automatically, when being interpreted. You may specify them in upper, lower or mixed case.

The contents of variables are not automatically uppercased.

These forms of PARSE will convert to uppercase:
```
ARG  /* data typed on the command line at execution time */
PULL /* data typed in response to a request from the terminal */
PARSE UPPER ARG /* data typed on the command line at execution time */
PARSE UPPER PULL /* data typed in response to a request from the term*/
```

These forms of PARSE will not convert to uppercase:
```
PARSE ARG  /* data typed on the command line at execution time */
PARSE PULL /* data typed in response to a request from the terminal */
```

To convert to uppercase: (A TRANSLATE with only one parameter, *string*, converts to upper case.)
```
NEW_STRING = TRANSLATE(string)
```

Also, to convert to uppercase:
```
NEW_STRING = UPPER(string)
```

&SYSDSN

This is used to determine if a dataset or PDS/PDSE is available.

```
/* CLST0023 TO ILLUSTRATE &SYSDSN */
 IF &SYSDSN(MY.DATASET.DATA) = OK THEN +
   DO
      WRITE DATASET IS AVAILABLE, DOING AN ALLOCATE
      ALLOCATE DDNAME(INFILE) SHR REUSE DSN(MY.DATASET.DATA)
   END
 ELSE WRITE &SYSDSN(MY.DATASET.DATA) /* ERROR MESSAGE */
```

&SYSINDEX

WRITE &SYSINDEX(*find-string,string2,start-pos*)
This gives you the position of *find-string* in *string2*, starting at *start-pos*. *Start-pos* defaults to 1.

```
/* CLST0024 TO ILLUSTRATE &SYSINDEX */
SET ALPHABET = ABCDEFGHIJKLMNOPQRSTUVWXYZ
WRITE &SYSINDEX(G,&ALPHABET,1)    /* GIVES 7 */

SET ALPHABET = ABCDEFGHIJKLMNOPQRSTUVWXYZ
WRITE &SYSINDEX(1,&ALPHABET,1)    /* NOT FOUND. GIVES 0*/

SET ALPHABET = ABCDEFGHIJKLMNOPQRSTUVWXYZ
WRITE &SYSINDEX(G,&ALPHABET,27)   /* GIVES 0 */
```

&SYSONEBYTE

Converts DBCDS data to character data, when there is an equivalent.
DBCS data cannot be shown here. The example code on the next entry, &SYSTWOBYTE, will illustrate a conversion to DBCS and back again.
See Supplement 4.

&SYSTWOBYTE

Converts character data to DBCDS data, when there is an equivalent. The converse of &SYSONEBYTE. This example program shows converting character data to DBCS and back again to character.

```
/* CLST0025 TO ILLUSTRATE &SYSONEBYTE AND &SYSTWOBYTE   */
/* DBCS DATA CAN NOT BE DISPLAYED HERE.                 */
/* THE FOLLOWING SHOWS A CONVERSION TO DBCS             */
/* AND BACK AGAIN TO CHARACTER DATA                     */
 WRITE &SYSONEBYTE(&SYSTWOBYTE(ABCD))
```

See Supplement 4.

&SYSDSN REXX Equivalent

The REXX function SYSDSN() is essentially the same as &SYSDSN. This example shows the parallels between the two.

```
/* REXX023 TO ILLUSTRATE SYSDSN */
 IF SYSDSN(MY.DATASET.DATA) = "OK" THEN
   DO
       SAY "DATASET IS AVAILABLE, DOING AN ALLOCATE"
       "ALLOCATE DDNAME(INFILE) SHR REUSE DSN(MY.DATASET.DATA)"
   END
 ELSE SAY SYSDSN(MY.DATASET.DATA) /* ERROR MESSAGE */
```

&SYSINDEX Equivalent in REXX

INDEX() is functionally equivalent to &SYSINDEX, but the syntax is different.
SAY INDEX(*string, find-string, start-pos*)

```
/* REXX PROGRAM REXX0024 TO ILLUSTRATE INDEX() */
ALPHABET = "ABCDEFGHIJKLMNOPQRSTUVWXYZ"
SAY INDEX(ALPHABET,"G",1)    /* GIVES 7 */

ALPHABET = "ABCDEFGHIJKLMNOPQRSTUVWXYZ"
SAY INDEX(ALPHABET,"1",1)    /* NOT FOUND. GIVES 0*/

ALPHABET = "ABCDEFGHIJKLMNOPQRSTUVWXYZ"
SAY INDEX(ALPHABET,"G",27)   /* GIVES 0 */
```

&SYSONEBYTE

The REXX function DBTODBCS will convert character data to DBCS.
```
/* REXX REXX0025 TO ILLUSTRATE DBCS */
OPTIONS "EXMODE"    /* REQUIRED BEFORE YOU CAN USE DBCS DATA */
DBCS_STRING2 = DBTODBCS("ABCD")
SAY DATATYPE(DBCS_STRING2,D)      "GIVES A 1, MEANING DBCS"
```
See Supplement 4.

&SYSTWOBYTE

The REXX function DBTOSBCS will convert DBCS to single byte.
```
OPTIONS "EXMODE"    /* REQUIRED BEFORE YOU CAN USE DBCS DATA */
/* THE CHARACTER AFTER OPEN   QUOTE IS HEX '0E'  */
/* THE CHARACTER BEFORE CLOSE QUOTE IS HEX '0F'  */
DBCS_STRING =  " D1F2D3 "
SINGLE_BYTE  = DBTOSBCS(DBCS_STRING)
SAY SINGLE_BYTE
```
See Supplement 4.

This page intentionally left blank

Chapter 4: The CONTROL Statement

Chapter 4 is about the CONTROL instruction that is used for debugging and for controlling the effect of a CLIST failure.

Chapter 4 contains:

Chapter 4: The CONTROL Statement

4.1 CONTROL Statement, General

CONTROL is a CLIST instruction. It talks to the CLIST interpreter. It affects instructions and commands that take place after the CONTROL statement is executed.

A subsequent CONTROL statement replaces the effect of the previous CONTROL statement.

You may specify more than one option on a CONTROL: CONTROL LIST CONLIST SYMLIST

4.2 CONTROL LIST

Causes TSO commands to be displayed after symbolic substitution is done. If you do not execute this command, the default action is the same as doing a CONTROL NOLIST.

```
CONTROL LIST     /* TSO commands are displayed*/
                 /* after symbolic substitution is done */
CONTROL NOLIST /* TSO commands are not displayed*/
                 /* after symbolic substitution is done */
```

You can achieve the same effect with &SYSLIST

```
SET SYSLIST = ON   /* same as CLIST control statement CONTROL LIST */
SET SYSLIST = OFF /* same as CLIST control statement CONTROL NOLIST */
```

4.3 CONTROL CONLIST

Causes CLIST statements to be displayed after symbolic substitution is done. If you do not execute this command, the default action is the same as doing a CONTROL NOCONLIST.

```
CONTROL CONLIST      /* CLIST statements are displayed*/
                     /*  after symbolic substitution is done */
CONTROL NOCONLIST    /* CLIST statements are not displayed*/
                     /* after symbolic substitution is done*/
```

You can achieve the same effect with &SYSCONLIST.

```
SET SYSCONLIST = ON   /* same as CONTROL CONLIST */
SET SYSCONLIST = OFF /* same as CONTROL NOCONLIST */
```

CONTROL Statement, General
Although REXX doesn't have a CONTROL statement, you can achieve the same effect most of the time with REXX functions and/or TSO commands.

CONTROL LIST Equivalent in REXX
CALL TRACE "C" is a close REXX equivalent for CLIST CONTROL LIST.

```
TRACE C
SAY TRACE()     /* GIVES CURRENT SETTING OF TRACE. NOT SAME AS CLIST */
CALL TRACE "C" /* DISPLAY RESULTS OF TSO COMMANDS */
CALL TRACE "OFF"    /* TURN OFF TRACING */
```

REXX TRACE has many more options that are not shown here, because there they work very differently from CLIST.

CONTROL CONLIST Equivalent in REXX
There is no exact equivalent for CONTROL CONLIST in REXX. You can achieve the same functionality using TRACE.

```
SAY TRACE()     /* GIVES CURRENT SETTING OF TRACE. NOT SAME AS CLIST */
CALL TRACE "R" /* DISPLAY RESULTS OF REXX INSTRUCTIONS */
CALL TRACE "I" /* DISPLAY INTERMEDIATE RESULTS OF INSTRUCTIONS */
CALL TRACE "OFF"    /* TURN OFF TRACING */
```

REXX TRACE has many more options that are not shown here, because there they work very differently from CLIST.

4.4 CONTROL SYMLIST

Causes CLIST statements to be displayed before symbolic substitution is done, I.E., as written. If you do not execute this command, the default action is the same as doing a CONTROL NOSYMLIST

```
CONTROL SYMLIST       /* CLIST statements are displayed*/
                      /* after symbolic substitution is done*/
CONTROL NOSYMLIST     /* CLIST statements s are not displayed*/
                      /* after symbolic substitution is done*/
```

You can achieve the same effect with &SYSSYMLIST

```
SET SYSSYMLIST = ON  /* same as CONTROL SYMLIST */
SET SYSSYMLIST = OFF /* same as CONTROL NOSYMLIST */
```

4.4 CONTROL END

This allows you to change the keyword used to delimit a DO – END sequence or a SELECT – END sequence. The default keyword is "END". This allows you to change it to something else, for example: "FINI".

If you use this, good programming practice dictates that it should be at the beginning of the CLIST, there should be only one CONTROL END, and it should apply to the entire CLIST. If you experience conflicts from the 8 possibilities mentioned just below, you should consider using CONTROL END.

This is used in CLISTs because "END" is ambiguous. "END" means several things:
1. It delimits a DO – END sequence
2. It delimits a DO UNTIL control structure
3. It delimits a DO WHILE control structure
4. It delimits a SELECT control structure
5. It delimits a subprocedure, and logically ends its execution
6. It is the subcommand that ends a Line Mode TSO Edit session
7. It is the subcommand that ends several other TSO commands
8. An "END" that is not being used for any of the above is equivalent to a CLIST EXIT instruction—it ends the CLIST. If the CLIST interpreter finds an "END" that is not matched with a DO, and is not used for any other purpose, it ends the CLIST.
   Good programming practice dictates that this should never happen.

You cannot change the meaning of "END" for numbers 6, 7 and 8, above.

For numbers 6 and 7, above, you can put the END between a DATA instruction and an ENDDATA instruction.

```
CONTROL END(FINI)
IF &A = 1 THEN +
    DO
    /* CODE */
    FINI
```

CONTROL SYMLIST REXX Equivalent

There is no exact equivalent for CONTROL SYMLIST in REXX. You can achieve the same functionality using TRACE.

```
SAY TRACE()      /* GIVES CURRENT SETTING OF TRACE. NOT SAME AS CLIST */
CALL TRACE "R"   /* DISPLAY RESULTS OF REXX INSTRUCTIONS */
CALL TRACE "I"   /* DISPLAY INTERMEDIATE RESULTS OF INSTRUCTIONS */
CALL TRACE "OFF"    /* TURN OFF TRACING */
```

REXX TRACE has many more options that are not shown here, because there they work very differently from CLIST.

CONTROL END

There is no equivalent to this in REXX. You cannot change the meaning of "END".
Here is what "END" can mean in a REXX program:

1. It delimits a DO – END sequence
2. It delimits a DO UNTIL control structure
3. It delimits a DO WHILE control structure
4. It delimits a SELECT control structure
5. N/A. RETURN delimits and ends a subroutine or function in REXX.
6. When placed in quotes, it is the subcommand that ends a Line Mode TSO Edit session
7. When placed in quotes, it is the subcommand that ends several other TSO commands
8. N/A. A superfluous "END" in your REXX program will be rejected as a syntax error, for an unmatched DO/END.

4.6 CONTROL MAIN

Protects the input stack. If an attention interrupt occurs, and you don't protect the input stack, the CLIST is terminated, along with all the instructions and commands that were going to be executed. (The input stack.) If you create an ATTN routine, and don't terminate the CLIST in it, you need a CONTROL MAIN or a CONTROL NOFLUSH instruction to protect the input stack.

```
CONTROL MAIN
ATTN +
    DO
      /* code */
    END
```

4.7 CONTROL NOFLUSH

Protects the input stack. If an attention interrupt occurs, the CLIST is terminated, along with all the instructions and commands that were going to be executed. (The input stack.)
If you create an ATTN routine, and don't terminate the CLIST in it, you need a CONTROL MAIN or a CONTROL NOFLUSH instruction to protect the input stack.

```
CONTROL NOFLUSH
ATTN +
    DO
      /* code */
    END
```

4.8 CONTROL MSG

Some TSO commands display messages that you don't want the user to see. An example of this is the "Not freed, is not allocated" message that is displayed when you do a FREE DDNAME TSO command that was not needed. Many old CLISTs were written before the appearance of the REUSE operand of the TSO ALLOCATE command, which makes it unnecessary to do a "just-in-case" FREE DDNAME.

```
CONTROL NOMSG
FREE DDNAME(INFILE)
CONTROL MSG
```

It is a good idea to restore the default, so that critical messages will be displayed. The TSO ALLOCATE command can fail for many reasons. Trying to handle all possible situations in a CLIST can lead to frustration. Hiding the error messages will make the situation worse.

CONTROL MAIN
There is no equivalent to CONTROL MAIN in REXX.

CONTROL NOFLUSH
There is no equivalent to CONTROL NOFLUSH in REXX.

CONTROL MSG
All the functionality of CONTROL MSG can be had by using REXX CALL MSG.

```
SAY MSG()
```
Returns:
```
ON    /* messages from TSO commands will be displayed*/
      /* (the default) */
OFF   /* messages from TSO commands will not be displayed */

CALL MSG "ON"   /* messages from TSO commands will be displayed*/
                /* (the default) */
CALL MSG "OFF" /* messages from TSO commands will not be displayed */
```

Some programmers use the style:
```
X = MSG(OFF)    or X = MSG("OFF")
```
instead of:
```
CALL MSG "OFF"
```

4.9 The syntax of the CONTROL Statement and REXX TRACE: Reference

CONTROL

CONTROL is used in a CLIST. It affects the execution and/or interpretation of instructions and commands that are chronologically after it.

If you want to affect the entire CLIST, place it at the beginning. You can cancel out its effect by subsequent CONTROL statements.

It is not the same as the ISPF CONTROL statement, which is not covered here.

CONTROL, with no keywords or operands, displays the options in effect at the time, for example:

```
FLUSH NOPROMPT NOLIST NOCONLIST NOSYMLIST MSG CAPS (the defaults).
```

The keywords or operands may not be variables. You may put one or more keywords on the statement.

Here are the keywords:
- **FLUSH** (the default)   The input stack (commands to be executed) will be flushed when an ERROR exception or attention interrupt occurs.
- **NOFLUSH**   The input stack (commands to be executed) will not be flushed when an ERROR exception or attention interrupt occurs.
- **PROMPT**   TSO will ask you for missing information on a TSO command or subcommand.
- **NOPROMPT** (the default)   TSO will not ask you for missing information on a TSO command or subcommand.
- **LIST**   TSO commands and subcommands are displayed as they are executed.
- **NOLIST** (the default)   TSO commands and subcommands are not displayed as they are executed.
- **CONLIST**   The CLIST interpreter displays CLIST instructions before they are executed, and after variables are resolved and arithmetic is done.
- **NOCONLIST** (the default)   The CLIST interpreter does not display CLIST instructions before they are executed, and after variables are resolved and arithmetic is done.
- **SYMLIST**   The CLIST interpreter displays CLIST instructions before they are executed, and before variables are resolved and arithmetic is done.
- **NOSYMLIST** (the default)   The CLIST interpreter does not display CLIST instructions before they are executed, and before variables are resolved and arithmetic is done.
- **MSG** (the default)   Error and informational messages from TSO commands and subcommands are displayed at the terminal.
- **NOMSG**   Error and informational messages from TSO commands and subcommands are not displayed at the terminal.
- **CAPS** (the default)   Data is converted to uppercase after it is entered.
- **NOCAPS** (same as ASIS)   Data is not converted from the case in which it is entered.
- **ASIS** (same as NOCAPS)   Data is not converted from the case in which it is entered.
- **MAIN**   This is the main CLIST that is executing. It cannot be deleted by an error exception in itself or in a CLIST that it executes.
- **END** (newvalue)   A way of changing the meaning of the keyword END in logic structures, such as IF, DO and SELECT

REXX TRACE
The REXX Trace instruction is used for debugging and to display values of variables as the program executes.

The format is TRACE ! or ? *trace-type*
! means "don't execute TSO commands or subcommands
? means turn or, or off, interactive debugging
trace-type is shown by the examples below.

- **TRACE !**   Nothing traced,
  Don't execute TSO commands

- **TRACE O** (Off)   Nothing traced

- **TRACE N** (Normal)   TSO cmds that fail/error out
  (The default)
  REXX verbs that fail

- **TRACE F** (Failure)   TSO commands that don't exist, or abend.

- **TRACE E** (Error)   TSO commands that don't work

- **TRACE !C**   Trace TSO commands,
  But don't execute them

- **TRACE C** (Commands) TSO commands

- **TRACE L** (Labels)   Labels only

- **TRACE A** (All)   Labels
  Commands
  REXX verbs

More on the next right-hand page.

The REXX trace is continued on the facing page.

TRACE continued from previous right-hand page
- **TRACE !R** (Results)   Labels
  Commands
  REXX verbs
  Any time a variable changes
  Don't execute TSO commands

- **TRACE R** (Results)   Labels
  Commands
  REXX verbs
  any time a variable changes

- **TRACE ?R** (Results)   Labels
  Commands
  REXX verbs
  Any time a variable changes
  With Interactive Debug

- **TRACE I** (Intermed)   Labels
  Commands
  REXX verbs
  Any time a variable changes
  Intermediate results
  Example: C = (4*3) + 2

- **TRACE !I** (Intermed)   Labels
  Commands
  REXX verbs
  Any time a variable changes
  Intermediate results
  Example: C = (4*3) + 2
  Don't execute TSO commands

- **TRACE ?I** (Intermed)   Labels
  Commands
  REXX verbs
  Any time a variable changes
  Intermediate results
  Example: C = (4*3) + 2
  With Interactive Debug

Chapter 4: The CONTROL Statement

This page intentionally left blank

Chapter 5: Conditional Statements

Chapter 5 is about the statements that allow your CLIST to make decisions. Both the IF and the SELECT are clear and structured.

Chapter 5 contains:

Chapter 5: Conditional Statements

5.1 IF
Basic form
The basic form of the IF is:

IF *condition* THEN *action1*
ELSE *action2*

Condition is a comparison of two terms. You may compare two literals or two variables, or one literal and one variable.

Complex conditions are possible, if you use AND or OR. See Chapter 5, Section 5.3.

Action1 and *action2* can be:

      one CLIST instruction or control statement

      one TSO command or subcommand

      null. Nothing. If there is nothing specified for an action, then nothing happens.

          It is not a syntax error, but it does make it more difficult to understand the program.

      A DO - END sequence

Physical format
The IF is all on one line, unless you continue with a + or -. The ELSE is on a separate line, with no preceding continuation character.

IF *condition* +
THEN *action1*
ELSE *action2*

```
SET A = 1
IF &A = 1 +
THEN WRITE IT IS EQUAL
ELSE WRITE IT IS NOT EQUAL
```

ELSE optional
The ELSE and its action are optional.

IF *condition* THEN *action1*

```
SET A = 1
IF &A = 1 +
THEN WRITE IT IS EQUAL
```

REXX IF
Basic Form
The basic form of the IF is:
IF condition then action1
ELSE action2

Condition is a comparison of two terms. You may compare two literals or two variables, or one literal and one variable.
Complex conditions are possible, if you use & or |. On the mainframe the character (|) is the solid vertical bar (hex 4F).

Action1 and *action2* can be:
>one REXX instruction or control statement
>one TSO command or subcommand
>NOP. Nothing. To do nothing on an outcome, code NOP. A null, or empty space, won't work.
>A DO - END sequence

Physical format
The IF is on one line, unless you continue with a comma. The ELSE is on a separate line, with no preceding continuation character.
IF *condition* THEN *action1*
ELSE *action2*

If you want to put the ELSE on the same line as the IF, you need a semicolon.
IF *condition* THEN *action1* ; ELSE *action2*

THEN can be on a separate line. No continuation character is needed.
IF *condition*
THEN *action1*
ELSE *action2*

ELSE optional
The ELSE and its action are optional.
IF *condition* THEN *action1*

```
A = 1
IF A = 1
THEN SAY "IT IS EQUAL"
```

Example of the IF:

```
/* CLST0026 TO ILLUSTRATE FORMAT OF IF, THEN AND ELSE */
/* THEN AND ELSE SPECIFIED */
SET SALARY = 100
WRITE PLEASE ENTER NAME   (JOE)
READ NAME
IF &NAME = JOE +
THEN SET SALARY = &SALARY * 2
ELSE SET  SALARY = &SALARY - 1
WRITE NEW SALARY IS &SALARY


/* NO ELSE */
SET SALARY = 100
WRITE PLEASE ENTER NAME    (JOE)
READ NAME
IF &NAME = JOE +
THEN SET SALARY = &SALARY * 2
WRITE NEW SALARY IS &SALARY


/* NULL THEN */
SET SALARY = 100
WRITE PLEASE ENTER NAME   (NOT JOE)
READ NAME
IF &NAME = JOE +
THEN
ELSE SET  SALARY = &SALARY - 1
WRITE NEW SALARY IS &SALARY


/* NULL THEN WITH UNSET VARIABLE WHOSE VALUE IS NULL */
SET SALARY = 100
WRITE PLEASE ENTER NAME (NOT JOE)
READ NAME
IF &NAME = JOE +
THEN &NULL
ELSE SET  SALARY = &SALARY - 1
WRITE NEW SALARY IS &SALARY
```

Example of REXX IF:

```
/* REXX0026 TO ILLUSTRATE FORMAT OF IF, THEN AND ELSE */
/* THEN AND ELSE SPECIFIED */
SALARY = 100
SAY "PLEASE ENTER NAME   (JOE)"
PULL NAME
IF NAME = "JOE"
THEN SALARY = SALARY * 2
ELSE SALARY = SALARY - 1
SAY "NEW SALARY IS" SALARY

/* NO ELSE */
SALARY = 100
SAY "PLEASE ENTER NAME    (JOE) "
PULL NAME
IF NAME = "JOE"
THEN SALARY = SALARY * 2
SAY "NEW SALARY IS" SALARY

/* NULL THEN */
SALARY = 100
SAY "PLEASE ENTER NAME   (NOT JOE) "
PULL NAME
IF NAME = "JOE"
THEN NOP
ELSE SALARY = SALARY - 1
SAY "NEW SALARY IS" SALARY

/* NULL THEN WITH UNSET VARIABLE WHOSE VALUE IS NULL */
/* YOU CAN'T DO THAT IN REXX, BUT NOP IS THE REXX EQUIVALENT */
SALARY = 100
SAY "PLEASE ENTER NAME (NOT JOE)"
PULL NAME
IF NAME = "JOE"
THEN NOP
ELSE SALARY = SALARY - 1
SAY "NEW SALARY IS" SALARY
```

More than one action on an outcome.

When you want to do more than 1 action on an outcome, you must use a DO – END sequence.

```
/* CLST0027 TO ILLUSTRATE DO - END SEQUENCES */
SET SALARY = 100
WRITE PLEASE ENTER NAME (JOE)
READ NAME
IF &NAME = JOE +
THEN DO /* NAME = JOE */
    SET SALARY = &SALARY * 2
    WRITE DOUBLING JOE'S SALARY
    WRITE NEW SALARY IS &SALARY
    END /* NAME = JOE */
ELSE DO /* NAME NE  JOE */
    SET  SALARY = &SALARY - 1
    WRITE REDUCING SALARY BY ONE
    WRITE NEW SALARY IS &SALARY
    END /* NAME NE  JOE */
```

Compound conditions.

Compound conditions are done with AND and OR or the equivalent symbols && and |. See Chapter 5, Section 5.3. Parentheses can be used to ensure that TSO interprets your code the way that you do.

```
/* CLST0028 TO ILLUSTRATE COMPOUND CONDITIONS */
/*COMPOUND CONDITION.  THEN AND ELSE SPECIFIED */
WRITE TODAY'S DATE IS &STR(&SYSSDATE)
SET SALARY = 100
WRITE PLEASE ENTER NAME (JOE)
READ NAME
IF &NAME = JOE  AND &STR(&SYSSDATE) GT &STR(21/06/09) +
THEN SET SALARY = &SALARY * 2
ELSE SET SALARY = &SALARY - 1
WRITE NEW SALARY IS &SALARY

/*COMPOUND CONDITION.  THEN AND ELSE SPECIFIED */
/*PARENTHESES ASSURE CORRECT INTERPRETATION */
SET SALARY = 100
WRITE PLEASE ENTER NAME   (JOE OR MARY)
READ NAME
IF (&NAME = JOE OR &NAME = MARY) +
    AND &STR(&SYSSDATE) GT &STR(21/06/09)+
THEN SET SALARY = &SALARY * 2
ELSE SET SALARY = &SALARY - 1
WRITE NEW SALARY IS &SALARY
```

Chapter 5: Conditional Statements

More than one action on an outcome in REXX

When you want to do more than 1 action on an outcome, you must use a DO – END sequence.
The example shows that there is an exact parallel between CLIST and REXX.

```
/* REXX0027 TO ILLUSTRATE DO - END SEQUENCES */
SALARY = 100
SAY "PLEASE ENTER NAME (JOE) "
PULL NAME
IF NAME = "JOE"
THEN DO /* NAME = JOE */
    SALARY = SALARY * 2
    SAY "DOUBLING JOE'S SALARY "
    SAY "NEW SALARY IS" SALARY
    END /* NAME = JOE */
ELSE DO /* NAME <>  JOE */
    SALARY = SALARY - 1
    SAY "REDUCING SALARY BY ONE "
    SAY "NEW SALARY IS" SALARY
    END /* NAME <>  JOE */
```

Compound conditions in REXX

Compound conditions are done with & and |. Parentheses can be used to ensure that TSO interprets your code the way that you do. (|). On the mainframe this character is the solid vertical bar (hex 4F).

```
/* REXX0028 TO ILLUSTRATE COMPOUND CONDITIONS */
/*COMPOUND CONDITION.  THEN AND ELSE SPECIFIED */
SAY "TODAY'S DATE IS" DATE(O)
SALARY = 100
SAY "PLEASE ENTER NAME (JOE)"
PULL NAME
IF NAME = "JOE"  & DATE(O)  > "21/06/09"
THEN SALARY = SALARY * 2
ELSE SALARY = SALARY - 1
SAY "NEW SALARY IS" SALARY

/*COMPOUND CONDITION.  THEN AND ELSE SPECIFIED */
/*PARENTHESES ASSURE CORRECT INTERPRETATION */
SALARY = 100
SAY "PLEASE ENTER NAME  (JOE OR MARY) "
PULL NAME
IF (NAME = "JOE" | NAME = MARY) ,
    & DATE(O)  > "21/06/09"
THEN SALARY = SALARY * 2
ELSE SALARY = SALARY - 1
SAY "NEW SALARY IS" SALARY
```

Nesting IF statements

Nesting works very well, to any reasonable level. Matching of DOs and ENDs should be done by careful indentation and commenting.

```
/* CLST0029 TO ILLUSTRATE NESTED IF */
WRITE PLEASE ENTER NAME AND DEPARTMENT (JOE DEPT1 OR DEPT2)
SET SALARY = 100
READ NAME DEPARTMENT
IF &NAME = JOE THEN +
    DO /* NAME = JOE */
        IF &DEPARTMENT = DEPT1 THEN +
        DO /* DEPT 1 */
         SET SALARY = &SALARY * 2
        END /* DEPT 1 */
      IF &DEPARTMENT = DEPT2 THEN +
        DO /* DEPT 2 */
         SET SALARY = &SALARY * 3
        END /* DEPT 2 */
    END /* NAME = JOE */

WRITE NEW SALARY IS &SALARY
```

Nesting IF Statements in REXX

This works the same way in REXX and CLIST.

```
/* REXX0029 TO ILLUSTRATE NESTED IF */
SAY "PLEASE ENTER NAME AND DEPARTMENT (JOE DEPT1 OR DEPT2)"
SALARY = 100
PULL NAME DEPARTMENT
IF NAME = "JOE" THEN
    DO /* NAME = JOE */
        IF DEPARTMENT = "DEPT1" THEN
        DO /* DEPT 1 */
         SALARY = SALARY * 2
        END /* DEPT 1 */
     IF DEPARTMENT = "DEPT2" THEN
        DO /* DEPT 2 */
         SALARY = SALARY * 3
        END /* DEPT 2 */
    END /* NAME = JOE */

SAY "NEW SALARY IS" SALARY
```

5.2 SELECT

SELECT is CLIST's case structure: several possibilities, each with a different outcome.
The first WHEN that comes true is the one executed. The remaining WHENs are ignored.
You may perform *one* action for each WHEN outcome. If you want to perform more than one action, you need to use a DO – END sequence, exactly as is done with the IF.
The parentheses around the condition on the WHEN are required.

OTHERWISE is the default, catch-all alternative. If all the WHENs are false, the OTHERWISE takes control and its action is executed. OTHERWISE is optional.
The END at the end is required, and matches the SELECT.
As with IF, compound conditions are possible.

There are two basic formats: SELECT without an expression and SELECT with an expression.

SELECT with no expression
You use a SELECT followed by one or more WHENs, each with a complete condition.

SELECT with an expression
Your SELECT contains an expression. Each WHEN has a possible value for the expression.

The general format of the SELECT with no expression
```
select
    when (condition) +
    action
    when (condition) +
    action

otherwise +
    action
end /* select */
```

Example:
```
/* CLST0030 TO ILLUSTRATE SELECT WITH NO EXPRESSION */
SET A = 2
SELECT
    WHEN (&A = 1) +
    WRITE A IS EQUAL TO 1
    WHEN (&A = 2) +
    WRITE A IS EQUAL TO 2
    WHEN (&A = 3) +
    WRITE A IS EQUAL TO 3
OTHERWISE +
    WRITE A WAS NOT EQUAL TO ANY OF THE VALUES
END /* SELECT */
```

SELECT in REXX

SELECT in REXX works essentially the same way as in CLIST. There is a slight difference in syntax: no continuation character is needed at the end of the WHEN line or the OTHEWISE line. The examples show the similarities and minor differences.

There is one format in REXX: SELECT without an expression.

SELECT with no expression

You use a SELECT followed by one or more WHENs, each with a complete condition.

The general format of the SELECT with no expression
```
select
    when (condition)
    then action
    when (condition)
    then  action

otherwise
    action
end /* select */
```

Example:
```
/* REXX0030 TO ILLUSTRATE SELECT WITH NO EXPRESSION */
A = 2
SELECT
    WHEN (A = 1)
    THEN SAY "A IS EQUAL TO 1"
    WHEN (A = 2)
    THEN SAY "A IS EQUAL TO 2"
    WHEN (A = 3)
    THEN SAY "A IS EQUAL TO 3 "
OTHERWISE
    SAY "A WAS NOT EQUAL TO ANY OF THE VALUES"
END /* SELECT */
```

SELECT, continued
The general format of the SELECT with an expression
select (expression)
  when (value) +
  action
  when (value) +
  action

otherwise +
  action
end /* select */

Examples:
```
/* CLST0031 TO ILLUSTRATE SELECT WITH AN EXPRESSION */
SET A = 2
SELECT (&A)
    WHEN (1) +
    WRITE A IS EQUAL TO 1
    WHEN (2) +
    WRITE A IS EQUAL TO 2
    WHEN (3) +
    WRITE A IS EQUAL TO 3
OTHERWISE +
    WRITE A WAS NOT EQUAL TO ANY OF THE VALUES
END /* SELECT */

/* CLST0032 TO ILLUSTRATE SELECT WITH A MORE COMPLEX EXPRESSION */
SET A = 2
SET B = 3
SELECT (&A + &B)
    WHEN (2) +
    WRITE TOTAL IS 2
    WHEN (3) +
    WRITE TOTAL IS 3
    WHEN (5) +
    WRITE TOTAL IS 5
OTHERWISE +
    WRITE TOTAL WAS NOT EQUAL TO ANY OF THE VALUES
END /* SELECT */
```

SELECT in REXX, continued
SELECT, in REXX, does not work with an expression

5.3 The Logical Operators

These are used with the conditional statements IF and SELECT. This information is repeated in Chapter 2.

=	or	EQ
¬=	or	NE
<	or	LT
>	or	GT
<=	or	LE
>=	or	GE
¬>	or	NG
¬<	or	NL

¬= or NE (¬ has the hex configuration of 5F on the mainframe.)

&& or AND

| or OR (| has the hex configuration of 4F on the mainframe.

Chapter 5: Conditional Statements

The Logical Operators in REXX

=   Equal. If numeric, when compared algebraically.
            (1.0 is equal to 001.000.)
            If not numeric, when padded with leading or trailing spaces.
            ("Sue" is equal to " Sue ".)
            Case is significant: "SUE" is not equal to "sue".

<>   Not equal, the negation of "=".
            Algebraic comparison and padding are performed.

><   Not equal, the negation of "=".
            Algebraic comparison and padding are performed.

\=   Not equal, the negation of "=".
            Algebraic comparison and padding are performed.

¬=   Not equal, the negation of "=". (¬ has the hex configuration of 5F)
            (The symbol "¬" may not be found on all keyboards.)
            Algebraic comparison and padding are performed.

^=   Not equal, the negation of "=".
            (The symbol "^" may not be found on all keyboards.)
            Algebraic comparison and padding are performed.

<   Less than. Algebraic comparison and padding are performed.

>   Greater than. Algebraic comparison and padding are performed.

<=   Less than or equal to. Algebraic comparison and padding are performed.

>=   Greater than or equal to. Algebraic comparison and padding are performed.

¬>   Not greater than. (The symbol "¬" may not be found on all keyboards.)
            Algebraic comparison and padding are performed.

\>   Not greater than. Algebraic comparison and padding are performed.

¬<   Not less than. (The symbol "¬" may not be found on all keyboards.)
            Algebraic comparison and padding are performed.

\<   Not less than. Algebraic comparison and padding are performed.

&   AND
| OR: either one, or both (| has the hex configuration of 4F on the mainframe.)
&&   Exclusive OR: one is true, not both.

This page intentionally left blank

Chapter 6: Looping

Chapter 6 is about the CLIST control structures that repeat. You can do something repeatedly as long as something is true, until something comes true, or until a value is equal to another value.

Chapter 6 contains:
    6.1 DO WHILE
    6.2 DO UNTIL
    6.3 DO incrementing a variable to a limit

Chapter 6: Looping

6.1 DO WHILE

This will continue to loop as long as a condition is true. When the condition is no longer true, the loop will not repeat any longer.

The END is required, and is matched with the DO. You may change the keyword from END to something else with the CONTROL END statement.

Be sure that the ending condition will happen! Trying to cancel your CLIST with PA1 or ATTN is not always successful, and sometimes leaves you in a situation that you cannot get out of without having to have your session cancelled.

The general form of the DO WHILE is:

```
DO WHILE condition
        /* action */
        /* action */
END
```

Examples:
```
/* CLST0033 TO ILLUSTRATE DO WHILE */
SET REPLY =  /* SET TO NULL */
DO WHILE &REPLY =
  WRITE PLEASE PRESS ENTER TO CONTINUE. ANYTHING ELSE TO STOP
  READ REPLY
END


/* CLST0034 TO ILLUSTRATE DO WHILE */
SET TOTAL = 0
DO WHILE &TOTAL < 10 /*(STOP WHEN NOT TRUE) */
    SET TOTAL = &TOTAL + 1
    /* ACTION */
    WRITE &TOTAL
END


/* CLST0035 TO ILLUSTRATE DO WHILE */
SET INDEX = 1
SET MAX   = 10
DO WHILE &INDEX < &MAX /*(STOP WHEN NOT TRUE) */
   SET INDEX = &INDEX + 1
   /* ACTION */
   WRITE &INDEX
END
```

DO WHILE in REXX
There is little difference between CLIST DO WHILE and REXX DO WHILE.

Examples:
```
/* REXX0033 TO ILLUSTRATE DO WHILE */
REPLY = "" /* SET TO NULL */
DO WHILE REPLY =   ""
  SAY "PLEASE PRESS ENTER TO CONTINUE. ANYTHING ELSE TO STOP"
  PULL REPLY
END

/* REXX0034 TO ILLUSTRATE DO WHILE */
TOTAL = 0
DO WHILE TOTAL < 10 /*(STOP WHEN NOT TRUE) */
   TOTAL = TOTAL + 1
   /* ACTION */
   SAY TOTAL
END

/* REXX0035 TO ILLUSTRATE DO WHILE */
INDEX = 1
MAX   = 10
DO WHILE INDEX < MAX /*(STOP WHEN NOT TRUE) */
   INDEX = INDEX + 1
   /* ACTION */
   SAY INDEX
END
```

6.2 DO UNTIL

The DO UNTIL executes at least one time, and stops when a condition comes true. (The WHILE stops when a condition is not true.)

The END is required, and is matched with the DO. You may change the keyword from END to something else with the CONTROL END statement. Be sure that the ending condition will come true! The general form of the DO UNTIL is:

DO UNTIL condition
       /* action */
       /* action */
END

Examples:

```
/* CLST0036 TO ILLUSTRATE DO UNTIL */
SET REPLY =   /* SET TO NULL */
DO UNTIL &REPLY = STOP /*(STOP WHEN TRUE) */
   WRITE ENTER STOP TO TERMINATE LOOP, OR SOMETHING ELSE TO CONTINUE
   READ REPLY
   WRITE THANK YOU FOR YOUR REPLY
END
```

```
/* CLST0037 TO ILLUSTRATE DO UNTIL */
SET TOTAL = 0
DO UNTIL &TOTAL = 10 /*(STOP WHEN TRUE) */
    SET TOTAL = &TOTAL + 1
    /* ACTION */
    WRITE &TOTAL
END
```

```
/* CLST0038 TO ILLUSTRATE DO UNTIL */
SET INDEX = 1
SET MAX   = 10
DO UNTIL &INDEX = &MAX /*(STOP WHEN TRUE) */
    SET INDEX = &INDEX + 1
    /* ACTION */
    WRITE &INDEX
END
```

```
/* CLST0039 TO ILLUSTRATE DO UNTIL */
SET STOP = NO
DO UNTIL &STOP = STOP
    WRITE IN THE LOOP
    TIME
    WRITE ENTER STOP TO STOP, ANYTHING ELSE TO CONTINUE
    READ STOP
END
```

DO UNTIL in REXX

There is little difference between CLIST DO UNTIL and REXX DO UNTIL.

Examples:
```
/* REXX0036 TO ILLUSTRATE DO UNTIL */
REPLY = "" /* SET TO NULL */
DO UNTIL REPLY = "STOP" /*(STOP WHEN TRUE) */
    SAY "ENTER STOP TO TERMINATE LOOP, OR SOMETHING ELSE TO CONTINUE"
    PULL REPLY
    SAY "THANK YOU FOR YOUR REPLY"
END


/* REXX0037 TO ILLUSTRATE DO UNTIL */
TOTAL = 0
DO UNTIL TOTAL = 10 /*(STOP WHEN TRUE) */
    TOTAL = TOTAL + 1
    /* ACTION */
    SAY TOTAL
END /* DO UNTIL */


/* REXX0038 TO ILLUSTRATE DO UNTIL */
INDEX = 1
MAX   = 10
DO UNTIL INDEX = MAX /*(STOP WHEN TRUE) */
    INDEX = INDEX + 1
    /* ACTION */
    SAY INDEX
END


/* REXX0039 TO ILLUSTRATE DO UNTIL */
STOP = "NO"
DO UNTIL STOP = "STOP"
    SAY "IN THE LOOP"
    "TIME"
    SAY "ENTER STOP TO STOP, ANYTHING ELSE TO CONTINUE"
    PULL STOP
END
```

6.3 DO incrementing a variable to a limit

DO can initialize a variable and increment it by 1 (or any other number), and stop the loop at a limit. Add a positive number and loop up to a positive limit that is actually greater than the initial value.

Alternatively, you can add a negative number and loop to a limit that is lower than the initial value. The limit, in this case, may be a negative number.

Both TO and BY are optional, and may also be used on a WHILE or an UNTIL. If you don't have a TO, then you must have an upper limit somewhere else in the loop.

If you don't have a BY, the default increment is 1.

```
/* CLST0040 DO INCREMENTING A VARIABLE TO A LIMIT */
WRITE &STR(INDEX = 1 TO 20 BY 1)
DO INDEX = 1 TO 20 BY 1
    WRITE &INDEX
END

WRITE
WRITE &STR(INDEX = 1 TO 20 BY 2)
DO INDEX = 1 TO 20 BY 2
    WRITE &INDEX
END

WRITE
WRITE &STR(INDEX = 10 TO -2 BY -1)
DO INDEX = 10 TO -2 BY -1
    WRITE &INDEX
END
```

DO incrementing a variable to a limit in REXX

Every CLIST feature has a direct equivalent in the REXX DO. The two work essentially the same way.

```
/* REXX0040 DO INCREMENTING A VARIABLE TO A LIMIT */
SAY "INDEX = 1 TO 20 BY 1"
DO INDEX = 1 TO 20 BY 1
     SAY INDEX
END

SAY
SAY "INDEX = 1 TO 20 BY 2"
DO INDEX = 1 TO 20 BY 2
     SAY INDEX
END

SAY
SAY "INDEX = 10 TO -2 BY -1"
DO INDEX = 10 TO -2 BY -1
     SAY INDEX
END
```

This page intentionally left blank

Chapter 7: Trapping Unexpected Conditions

Chapter 7 is about what you can do when something unexpected happens.

Some error conditions will normally terminate your program, or will continue your program when you don't want it to continue. The user may press PA1 or ATTN, hoping to stop the program.

REXX has many more possibilities than CLIST, but REXX traps are more complex than CLIST traps.

The final section of this chapter has additional details about the syntax of the CLIST instructions and their REXX counterparts.

Chapter 7 contains:

Chapter 7: Trapping Unexpected Conditions

7.1 ATTN

If you want to regain control when the user presses the PA1 or the ATTN key, you can put an ATTN routine in your program.

ATTN routines cannot solve all problems that your CLIST may encounter. Consider them as a way to clean up and exit more or less gracefully from an unending loop, or an error exception, or to give the user a chance to decide if he or she wants to terminate the CLIST, as pressing PA1/ATTN implies.

Considerations:

- Must be physically and chronologically before the code that you want it to influence.
- You need a CONTROL MAIN or a CONTROL NOFLUSH in your CLIST, to prevent the PA1/ATTN from ending your program.
- &LASTCC contains the code from the last instruction executed outside of the ATTN routine.
- The ATTN routine is in effect until you execute another one, or do ATTN OFF.
- The interactions of attention interrupts, TSO, ISPF, ATTN routines and file IO are complex. Attempting to solve all problems and to handle all situations often leads to program complexity and frustration.
- If the program is currently executing an ERROR routine, control will not go to your ATTN routine.

What can be in the ATTN routine?

- CLIST instructions
- A maximum of one TSO command or subcommand
- An EXIT instruction, which ends the CLIST
- A RETURN instruction, which returns to the instruction or TSO command *after* the one executing when PA1/ATTN was pressed. (Do you know for sure which instruction it was on?)
- A null line, I.E., a line containing a null instruction. For example, a variable containing null, as the only thing on the line that is executed. This returns control to the instruction that was executing when the user pressed PA1/ATTN. (If it caused the user to interrupt, do you want to return control to it?)
- File closing statements for datasets that you are reading or writing.
- TSO FREE commands, to release datasets that you are reading or writing.

See the example of an ATTN routine on the next left-hand page.

The REXX HALT routine

REXX HALT, like CLIST ATTN, gets control when the user presses PA1 or ATTN.
It doesn't function exactly the same way as CLIST ATTN. Also, TSO processes attention interrupts differently under CLIST and under REXX. Thorough testing is essential, but you can't test for all situations.

Considerations:

- The HALT trap is normally placed at the physical end of the program. You must make sure that the flow of control does not *fall into* a HALT trap—you can do this by placing an EXIT before the first trap.
- RC is probably not useful in a HALT trap, since it is the return code from the last TSO command executed OR the error code indicating a REXX syntax error.
- You activate the HALT trap by executing code that says: **SIGNAL ON HALT**
- You de-activate the HALT trap by executing code that says: **SIGNAL OFF HALT**
- The HALT trap is in effect until you execute another one, or do **SIGNAL OFF HALT.**

What can be in the HALT trap?

- REXX instructions
- TSO commands or subcommands
- An EXIT instruction, which ends the program (Implies that you SIGNALled the trap. However, it will end the program even if you CALLed the trap).
- A RETURN instruction, which returns to the instruction or TSO command *after* the one executing when PA1/ATTN was pressed. (Do you know for sure which instruction it was on?) (Valid only if you CALLed the trap).
- File closing statements for datasets that you are reading or writing.
- TSO FREE commands, to release datasets that you are reading or writing.

See the example of a HALT trap on the next right-hand page.

<u>Example of an ATTN routine.</u>

```
/* CLST0041 TO ILLUSTRATE ATTN ROUTINE */
SET &NULL =
ATTN +
  DO
    WRITE YOU HIT ATTN/PA1!
    WRITE DO YOU WANT TO CONTINUE OR STOP?
    WRITE ENTER STOP OR ANYTHING ELSE TO CONTINUE
    READ CS
    IF &CS EQ STOP THEN EXIT
    WRITE ENTER YOUR NAME NOW
    &NULL  /* REEXECUTE STATEMENT THAT WAS INTERRUPTED (READ) */
  END /* ATTN DO */

WRITE PLEASE ENTER YOUR NAME
READ NAME
WRITE THANK YOU, &NAME, FOR ENTERING YOUR NAME SUCCESSFULLY
```

Example of a REXX HALT routine

```
/* REXX0041 TO ILLUSTRATE INTERRUPT PROCESSING */
CALL ON HALT /* CALL IMPLIES THAT CONTROL WILL COME BACK*/
SAY "PLEASE ENTER YOUR NAME"
PULL NAME
SAY "THANK YOU," NAME "FOR ENTERING YOUR NAME SUCCESSFULLY"

EXIT /* LOGICAL END OF PROGRAM. NEEDED BEFORE ROUTINES */

HALT:
    SAY "YOU HIT ATTN/PA1!        "
    SAY "DO YOU WANT TO CONTINUE OR STOP? "
    SAY "ENTER 'CONTINUE' OR 'STOP' "
    PULL CS
    IF CS = "CONTINUE" THEN DO
      SAY "ENTER YOUR NAME NOW"
      PULL NAME
      RETURN
      END
    IF CS = "STOP" THEN EXIT
```

7.2 ERROR

If a TSO command or subcommand or a CLIST instruction (but not a subprocedure) executes and gives back a non-zero return code, it is considered an error exception, and you may gain control in an ERROR routine. They are useful when TSO commands don't produce the desired results, and you want to ignore or handle the error exception. For example, a missing dataset.

Note: FREE and DELETE don't kick you out of the CLIST when you specify incorrect information.

Considerations:
- Must be physically and chronologically before the code that you want it to influence.
- You need a CONTROL MAIN or a CONTROL NOFLUSH in your CLIST, to prevent the error exception from ending your program.
- &LASTCC contains the code from the last instruction executed outside of the ERROR routine.
- The ERROR routine is in effect until you execute another one, or do ERROR OFF.
- When reading a file, the end-of-file exception is considered an error: it returns a code of 200, which you can recognize, and use it to stop the loop that reads the file.
- With ERROR OFF, TSO commands or subcommands with a non-zero return code, and program abends cause the CLIST to terminate.
- With ERROR OFF, CLIST statements and arithmetic evaluations that fail cause the CLIST to terminate. In my opinion, it's best to let the CLIST terminate in these situations.

What can be in the ERROR routine?
- CLIST instructions
- One or more TSO commands or subcommands
- An EXIT instruction, which ends the CLIST
- A RETURN instruction, which returns to the instruction or TSO command *after* the one executing when the error exception was raised.
- File closing statements for files that you are reading or writing.
- TSO FREE commands, to release datasets that you are reading or writing.

See the example of an ERROR routine on the next left-hand page.

ERROR in REXX

REXX ERROR is similar, but not exactly the same as CLIST ERROR. Note the differences:
REXX ERROR is triggered by a known TSO or ISPF command that works incorrectly or a TSO or ISPF command that gives a non-zero return code. It's also triggered by (if you don't have a REXX FAILURE trap) an unknown TSO command or subcommand, or a TSO or ISPF command, or program that abends.

Considerations:

- The ERROR trap is normally placed at the physical end of the program. You must make sure that the flow of control does not fall into a HALT trap—you can do this by placing an EXIT before the first trap.
- RC contains the code from the last TSO or ISPF command executed outside of the ERROR routine.
- The ERROR routine is in effect until you activate another one, or do ERROR OFF.
- You activate the ERROR trap by executing code that says: SIGNAL ON ERROR, or CALL ON ERROR.
- You de-activate the ERROR trap by executing code that says: SIGNAL OFF ERROR or CALL OFF ERROR.
- When reading a file one record at a time, the end-of-file exception returns a code of 2, which you can recognize, and use it to stop the loop that reads the file. You do not need an ERROR TRAP to process the end of file exception.
- With ERROR OFF, TSO commands or subcommands with a non-zero return code, and program or command abends, do not cause the REXX program to terminate.

What can be in the ERROR trap?

- REXX instructions
- One or more TSO commands or subcommands
- An EXIT instruction, which ends the program
- A RETURN instruction, which returns to the instruction or TSO command after the one executing when the error exception was raised (Valid only if you CALLed the trap).
- File closing statements for datasets that you are reading or writing.
- TSO FREE commands, to release datasets that you are reading or writing.

See the example of an ERROR trap on the next right-hand page.

```
/* CLST0042 TO ILLUSTRATE ERROR ROUTINE */
/* A TSO ALLOCATE FAILS, DUE TO WRONG DSN */
/* CONTROL GOES TO ERROR ROUT., WHERE USER IS ASKED FOR GOOD DSN */
 CONTROL LIST       /* TO SHOW COMMAND BEING EXECUTED */
 CONTROL NOFLUSH /* WITHOUT THIS, ALLOC BELOW KICKS OUT OF CLIST */
 ERROR +
   DO
     WRITE CAN'T ALLOCATE FILE
     WRITE DO YOU WANT TO ENTER A VALID DSN?
     READ YN
     IF &YN NE YES THEN EXIT
     WRITE ENTER VALID DSN
     READ DSN
     ALLOCATE DDNAME(INFILE) SHR REUSE DSN(&DSN)
     RETURN /* GO TO STATEMENT AFTER ONE THAT SENT HERE */
 END /* END OF ERROR ROUTINE */

 ALLOCATE DDNAME(INFILE) SHR REUSE DSN(ABC.NOTHERE.DATA)
```

```
/* REXX0042 TO ILLUSTRATE ERROR TRAP */
/* A TSO ALLOCATE FAILS, DUE TO WRONG DSN */
/* CONTROL GOES TO ERROR TRAP, WHERE PROGRAM ASKS FOR A GOOD DSN */

CALL ON ERROR
"ALLOCATE DDNAME(INFILE) SHR REUSE DSN(ABC.NOTHERE.DATA)"
CALL OFF ERROR
EXIT

/* FURTHER DOWN THE PROGRAM */
ERROR:
     SAY "CAN'T ALLOCATE FILE"
     SAY "DO YOU WANT TO ENTER A VALID DSN?"
     PULL YN
     IF YN <> "YES" THEN EXIT
     SAY "ENTER VALID DSN"
     PULL DSN
     "ALLOCATE DDNAME(INFILE) SHR REUSE DSN("DSN")"
     RETURN /* GO TO STATEMENT AFTER ONE THAT SENT HERE */
```

7.3 More Details on the Syntax of CLIST ATTN and ERROR, and REXX HALT and ERROR.

CLIST ATTN
Considerations for ATTN routines.

- If you don't have an ATTN routine, and the user presses PA1 or ATTN, the CLIST is terminated.
- You can write an ATTN routine that will gain control if the user presses PA1 or ATTN. It is not necessary to have a CONTROL NOFLUSH or a CONTROL MAIN for the ATTN routine to take effect.
- Place the ATTN routine in your program so that it is executed before the code that you want it to influence. It is not a subprocedure, and it is not placed at the physical end of the CLIST.
- To deactivate an ATTN routine, execute ATTN OFF

The format of the ATTN routine is:
```
ATTN +
    DO
            /* instructions */
    END
```

What can you put in the ATTN routine?

- You may execute a maximum of one TSO command or subcommand in an ATTN routine.
- A null line in the ATTN routine will return control to the instruction or command that was executing when the attention interrupt occurred.
- To execute a null line, you may use code like this:
```
SET NULLLINE =
&NULLLINE
```
- An EXIT will end the CLIST.
- A RETURN will send control to the instruction after the one that was executing when the attention interrupt occurred.
- You may want to close any files that were open, and FREE any allocations that you have done.

REXX HALT

Considerations for HALT traps.

- If you don't have a HALT trap, and the user presses PA1 or ATTN, you see the message:
  `ENTER HI TO END, A NULL LINE TO CONTINUE, OR AN IMMEDIATE COMMAND+` –
  if you reply **HI**, the program is terminated.
- You can write a HALT trap that will gain control if the user presses PA1 or ATTN.
- To activate the HALT trap, execute one of the following:
  CALL ON HALT (allows you to RETURN)
  or
  SIGNAL ON HALT (assumes you will EXIT)
- To deactivate a HALT trap, execute **SIGNAL OFF HALT** or **CALL OFF HALT**

The format of the HALT trap is:

```
HALT:
      /* instructions */
RETURN or EXIT
```

What can you put in the HALT trap?

- You may execute REXX instructions and TSO commands or subcommands in an HALT trap.
- An EXIT will end the program.
- A RETURN will send control to the instruction after the one that was executing when the error occurred.
- You may want to close any files that were open, and FREE any allocations that you have done.
- You may display the line number of the instruction that was executing: the reserved variable SIGL contains the line number
- You may display the instruction that was executing: the function SOURCELINE(SIGL) returns the text of the line of code that was executing.

CLIST ERROR
Considerations for ERROR routines
- If you don't have an ERROR routine, and a CLIST instruction or TSO command/subcommand returns a non-zero code, the CLIST is terminated. (A subprocedure that returns a non-zero code will not send you to an ERROR routine.)
- Possible ERROR exceptions:
    - TSO command with incorrect keywords
    - TSO command that can't find requested dataset (but not DELETE or FREE)
    - TSO command that doesn't exist
    - a TSO command or a program that abends
    - bad arithmetic operands (trying to add character data)
    - syntax error
- You can write an ERROR routine that will gain control if an ERROR exception occurs. It makes no sense to try to recover from a syntax error or bad arithmetic operands
- Place the ERROR routine in your program so that it is executed before the code that you want it to influence. It is not a subprocedure, and it is not placed at the physical end of the CLIST.
- A **CONTROL NOFLUSH** is needed for control to go to the ERROR routine in case of error
- To deactivate an ERROR routine, execute **ERROR OFF**
- &LASTCC contains the return code from the failing instruction or command

The format of the ERROR routine is:
```
CONTROL NOFLUSH
ERROR +
    DO
            /* instructions */
    END
```

What can you put in the ERROR routine?

- You may execute TSO commands or subcommands in an ERROR routine.
- An EXIT will end the CLIST.
- A RETURN will send control to the instruction after the one that was executing when the error occurred.
- You may want to close any files that were open, and FREE any allocations that you have done.

REXX ERROR
Considerations for ERROR traps
- If you don't have an ERROR trap, and a TSO command/subcommand returns a non-zero code, the program is *not* terminated.
- Possible ERROR exceptions:
- TSO command with incorrect keywords
- TSO command that can't find requested dataset
- TSO command that doesn't exist (sends to a FAILURE trap, if there is one.)
- a TSO command or a program abends (sends to a FAILURE trap, if there is one.)

- You can write an ERROR trap that will gain control if an ERROR exception occurs.
- Place the ERROR trap at the physical end of your program, preceded by an EXIT, so that control does not flow into the ERROR trap.
- To activate the ERROR trap, execute one of the following:
  CALL ON ERROR (allows you to RETURN)
  or
  SIGNAL ON ERROR (assumes you will EXIT)
- To deactivate an ERROR trap, execute **SIGNAL OFF ERROR** or **CALL OFF ERROR**
- RC contains the return code from the command with the problem

The format of the ERROR trap is:

```
ERROR:
      /* instructions */
RETURN or EXIT
```

What can you put in the ERROR trap?

- You may execute REXX instructions and TSO commands or subcommands in an ERROR trap.
- An EXIT will end the program.
- A RETURN will send control to the instruction after the one that was executing when the error occurred (if you did a CALL).
- You may want to close any files that were open, and FREE any allocations that you have done.
- Display the line number with the error: the reserved variable SIGL contains the line number of the command with the error
- Display the line in error: the function SOURCELINE(SIGL) returns the text of the line of code that produced the error
- Display the return code of the command that produced the error: the reserved variable RC contains the return code.

This page intentionally left blank

Chapter 8: Transfer of Control Statements

Chapter 8 is about how you can change the flow of execution in your program. You will find the unstructured transfer of control GOTO, and the structured subroutine invocation SYSCALL. Three instructions that return control are here too: EXIT, RETURN and END.

Chapter 8 contains:

8.1 GOTO

You can GOTO a label. (See Chapter 2, Section 2.13). You may not GOTO a subprocedure label. You may not GOTO out of a subprocedure while you are in it.

Example:
```
/* CLIST CLST0004 TO SHOW LABELS */
GOTO HERE
/* CODE */
/* CODE */

HERE: +
WRITE AFTER THE LABEL HERE
/* CODE */

GOTO THERE
/* CODE */
/* CODE */

THERE: WRITE AFTER THE LABEL THERE
/* CODE */

/* NO EXIT IS NEEDED BECAUSE CONTROL DOESN'T GO TO A SUBPROCEDURE */
/* EXCEPT THROUGH A SYSCALL */
MYSUBPROCEDURE: +
SET A = 1 + 2
RETURN
```

You may GOTO a variable containing a valid label. This is possible only in an interpreted language, like CLIST. Using it excessively will not win you admiration from your fellow programmers.

```
/* CLST0043 GOTO LABEL IN VARIABLE */
WRITE WHICH LABEL DO YOU WANT TO GO TO? (LABEL1, LABEL2, LABEL3)
READ LABEL
IF &LABEL = THEN EXIT /* STOP IF NOTHING ENTERED */
GOTO &LABEL
EXIT

LABEL1: +
WRITE IN LABEL1
EXIT
LABEL2: +
WRITE IN LABEL2
EXIT
LABEL3:+
WRITE IN LABEL3
EXIT
```

GOTO Equivalent in REXX

REXX has the SIGNAL *label* instruction, as an unconditional transfer of control. If you are converting an old CLIST that uses GOTO frequently, it will be difficult to convert.

SIGNAL won't work right if you use it to "go to" outside of a logic structure, or to transfer control inside a logic structure.

Example:
```
/* REXX PROGRAM REXX0004 TO SHOW LABELS */
SIGNAL HERE
/* CODE */
/* CODE */
HERE:
SAY "AFTER THE LABEL HERE"
/* CODE */

SIGNAL THERE
THERE:
SAY "AFTER THE LABEL THERE"

EXIT /* EXIT NEEDED SO CONTROL DOESN'T FALL INTO SUBROUTINE */

MYSUBROUTINE:
A = 1 + 2
RETURN
```

If you really want to go to a variable containing a valid label in REXX, you can code SIGNAL VALUE.
```
/* REXX REXX0043 SIGNAL A LABEL IN A VARIABLE */
SAY "WHICH LABEL DO YOU WANT TO GO TO? (LABEL1, LABEL2, LABEL3)"
PULL LABEL
IF LABEL = "" THEN EXIT
TRACE C
SIGNAL VALUE LABEL
EXIT
LABEL1:
SAY "IN LABEL1"
EXIT
LABEL2:
SAY "IN LABEL2"
EXIT
LABEL3:
SAY "IN LABEL3"
EXIT
```

8.2 SYSCALL

SYSCALL is used to transfer control temporarily to a subprocedure (see the next chapter for subprocedures). Control goes to the label of the subprocedure, and comes back to the statement after SYSCALL, when the subprocedure issues a RETURN or an END statement.

You may pass data on the SYSCALL instruction to the subprocedure. The subprocedure picks up the data on its PROC statement. The data may be literal strings, numbers or variables. The variables are resolved, and the resolved results are passed to the subprocedure.

```
SYSCALL MY_SUBPROC1                 /* call without parameters */
SET SALARY = 1000
SYSCALL MY_SUBPROC2 joe dept4 &salary /* call with parameters */
```

Note that a variable with a value of null will cause an error. The subprocedure's PROC statement specifies how many items must be passed to it on a SYSCALL. A null variable is nothing, so it doesn't count as an item being passed.

SYSCALL Equivalent in REXX

REXX CALL invokes a user-written subroutine, an external function, a built-in function, or an exception trap (ERROR, FAILURE, HALT, NOVALUE). REXX CALL is not in quotes. "CALL" is the TSO command that executes a compiled program on a program PDS/PDSE.

The REXX equivalent to a CLIST subprocedure is the REXX subroutine. You invoke the REXX subroutine with a CALL instruction. Control goes to the label of the subroutine, and comes back to the statement after the CALL, when the subroutine issues a RETURN statement.

You may pass data on the CALL instruction to the subroutine. The subroutine picks up the data on its ARG or PARSE ARG instruction. The data may be literal strings, numbers or variables. The variables are resolved, and the resolved results are passed to the subroutine.

```
CALL MY_SUBPROC1                    /* call without parameters */
SALARY = 1000
CALL MY_SUBPROC2 joe dept4 &salary /* call with parameters */
```

Notice that the data items are not separated with commas. They are delimited by spaces, just as for CLIST.

However, I generally separate the data items with commas, and also separate the variables on the ARG statement with commas. I'm not doing it here, to make the code more like the CLIST example. (Both ways work.)

A variable with a value of null will not raise an error.

8.3 EXIT

The CLIST instruction EXIT terminates your CLIST program wherever it is encountered. You may specify an integer on the EXIT instruction. That number is passed to the caller. If the caller is TSO, TSO sees the number as a return code from the CLIST. If the caller is another CLIST, the calling CLIST can see the number in the variables &LASTCC and &MAXCC. If the caller is a REXX program, the REXX program can see the number in the reserved variable RC.

If you want to exit from the current CLIST and from any calling CLIST, code EXIT QUIT.

However, if the CLIST calling yours has a CONTROL MAIN or a CONTROL NOFLUSH instruction in effect, control returns to that CLIST.

This information is duplicated in Chapter 2 Section 2.17.

```
EXIT                   /* terminates the program */
EXIT CODE(12)          /* terminates the program, passing 12 to the caller*/
EXIT QUIT              /* terminates the program, and all calling CLISTs,*/
                       /* unless one has CONTROL MAIN or CONTROL NOFLUSH */
EXIT CODE(12) QUIT     /* terminates the program, and all calling CLISTs,*/
                       /* unless one has CONTROL MAIN or CONTROL NOFLUSH */
                       /* and passes 12 to the caller */
```

8.4 RETURN

RETURN in used in CLIST subprocedures to send a number back to the main part of the CLIST, immediately after the SYSCALL that invoked the subprocedure. It ends the subprocedure. It can send back a number and a number only. (It may be in a variable). The number is visible right after the SYSCALL in &LASTCC and &MAXCC. A non-zero does not send control to an ERROR routine.

It ends the subprocedure and sends control back to the instruction after the SYSCALL. END also ends the subprocedure, but doesn't send back a return code.

(Inside of a subprocedure:)
```
RETURN CODE(12)
```

(Main part of program:)
```
SYSCALL MY_SUB
WRITE &LASTCC WAS RETURN CODE FROM SUBPROCEDURE
```

EXIT to End your Program in REXX

EXIT terminates your REXX program wherever it is encountered. You may specify an integer on the EXIT instruction. That number is passed to the caller. If the caller is TSO, TSO sees the number as a return code from the program. If the caller is CLIST, the calling CLIST can see the number in the variables &LASTCC and &MAXCC. If the caller is a REXX program, the REXX program can see the number in the reserved variable RC.

There is no equivalent to CLIST EXIT QUIT.

```
EXIT                    /* terminates the program */
EXIT 12                 /* terminates the program, passing 12 to the caller*/
```

RETURN

In REXX, RETURN is the way you return control to your caller from inside a subroutine, user-written function, or exception trap (ERROR, FAILURE, HALT, NOVALUE).

In a subroutine or user-written function you can pass back a number, a character string or the contents of a variable. The main part of the program sees the returned information in the reserved variable RESULT.

It ends the subroutine and sends control back to the instruction after the CALL.

(Inside of a subroutine:)
```
RETURN "THE RESULT OF THE CALCULATION IS " VARIABLE
```

(Main part of program:)
```
CALL MY_SUB
SAY "SUBROUTINE RETURNED " RESULT
```

8.5 END

END means many different things, depending on the context. (If the CLIST programmer commented each use of END that is not immediately obvious, consider yourself lucky.)

"END" means several things:
1. It delimits a DO – END sequence
2. It delimits a DO UNTIL control structure
3. It delimits a DO WHILE control structure
4. It delimits a SELECT control structure
5. It delimits a subprocedure, and logically ends its execution
6. It is the subcommand that ends a Line Mode TSO Edit session
7. It is the subcommand that ends several other TSO commands
8. An "END" that is not being used for any of the above is equivalent to a CLIST EXIT instruction—it ends the CLIST. If the CLIST interpreter finds an "END" that is not matched with a DO, and is not used for any other purpose, it ends the CLIST. Good programming practice dictates that this should never happen.

You cannot change the meaning of "END" for numbers 6, 7 and 8, above.

For numbers 6 and 7, above, you can put the END between a DATA instruction and an ENDDATA instruction.

Numbers 6, 7 and 8, above, are actual transfer of control statements. The others are delimiters of logic structures.

Number 5 is a transfer of control statement, and a logic delimiter.

Each of the above 8 possibilities are covered elsewhere in this book. Here is an example of number 8: the END that ends your program.

```
/* CLST0044 TO ILLUSTRATE THE END THAT ENDS THE PROGRAM */
/* THIS SHOULD NEVER BE ALLOWED TO HAPPEN.               */
/* INSTEAD, THE LOGICAL END OF YOUR PROGRAM SHOULD BE    */
/* EXIT                                                  */
WRITE THIS IS JUST BEFORE THE END STATEMENT
END
WRITE THIS IS RIGHT AFTER THE END STATEMENT (NEVER GET HERE)
```

END in REXX

Here is what "END" can mean in a REXX program:

1. It delimits a DO – END sequence
2. It delimits a DO UNTIL control structure
3. It delimits a DO WHILE control structure
4. It delimits a SELECT control structure
5. N/A. RETURN delimits and ends a subroutine or function in REXX.
6. When placed in quotes, it is the subcommand that ends a Line Mode TSO Edit session
7. When placed in quotes, it is the subcommand that ends several other TSO commands
8. N/A. A superfluous "END" in your REXX program will be rejected as a syntax error, for an unmatched DO/END.

```
/* REXX REXX0044 */
SAY "A SUPERFLUOUS 'END' IN A REXX PROGRAM IS A SYNTAX ERROR"
SAY "THIS PROGRAM WILL NOT EXECUTE, BECAUSE OF THE ERROR"
SAY "THIS IS JUST BEFORE THE END STATEMENT"
END
SAY "THIS IS RIGHT AFTER THE END STATEMENT (NEVER GET HERE)"
```

8.6 Additional information on the Syntax of SYSCALL and CALL.
CLIST SYSCALL

- SYSCALL implies that control will return when the subprocedure ends. The subprocedure ends by reaching the END instruction that corresponds to the subprocedure definition, or by a RETURN instruction.
- The flow of execution continues with the instruction or command after the SYSCALL
- SYSCALL invokes a subprocedure contained in your program.
- You can optionally pass one or more parameters to the subprocedure on the SYSCALL. The parameters can be character strings, variables or built-in functions. None of them may be blank, or contain a blank, or a null (zero characters.)

REXX CALL

- CALL implies that what you call will do a RETURN
- The flow of execution continues with the instruction or command after the CALL
- You may CALL:
  an internal subroutine (there are no external subroutines)
  an internal user-written function
  an external user-written function
  a built-in function
  an exception trap (HALT, ERROR, FAILURE, NOVALUE)
- it makes no sense to CALL a SYNTAX trap)
- A function (built-in or user-written) can be invoked in this format:
  THE_LENGTH = LENGTH(CHARACTER-STRING)
  (a function always returns something on its RETURN instruction
  and always receives a value passed to it through its ARG instruction)
- If you CALL a subroutine, it may return a value (number, character string) to you on its RETURN instruction
  you see the value in the reserved variable RESULT
- If you CALL a function, it will return a value (number, character string) to you on its RETURN instruction
  you see the value in the reserved variable RESULT
- Putting the name that you CALL in quotes forces REXX to execute only a built-in or an external function, bypassing any internal function or routine with the same name.
- To distinguish the TSO command CALL from the REXX CALL, enclose the TSO command in quotes:
  "CALL MYPROG.LIB(PROGRAMA)"
- You can pass one or more parameters on the CALL. The parameters can be character strings, variables or built-in functions. They may contain blanks or nulls (zero characters.)

This page intentionally left blank

Chapter 9: Writing Subprocedures

Chapter 9 is about writing CLIST subprocedures, logic structures that are logically equivalent to REXX subroutines.

Chapter 9 contains:

Chapter 9: Writing Subprocedures

9.1 Purpose of Subprocedures
- Subprocedures are used to create reusable code that you can reference and execute one or more times, from one or more places in the physical program in which they are found. They can be used for convenience: to contain code that you need to execute several times. They can be used as generic code: allowing you to specify a different input each time that you use them, knowing that the code will work the same way each time.
- Subprocedures make it easier to write understandable code. You can make the critical logic of your program short, clean and easy to understand. Transfers of control from distant places in your program lead to programs that are difficult to understand and to maintain.

9.2 Capabilities of Subprocedures
- CLIST subprocedures can receive input parameters (strings of data or variables), or can be executed without input parameters.
- Subprocedures can execute CLIST instructions and/or TSO commands.
- Subprocedures can pass a number (a return code) back to the instruction after the one that invoked them, or they can return control without a number.
- They can pass information (a number or a character string, generally the result of the subprocedure's processing) back in a specific variable that you choose by means of NGLOBAL or SYSREF. Since all variables are hidden from the main part of the CLIST, by default, the subprocedure, acting in concert with the SYSCALL, PROC and SYSREF instructions, can designate one or more variables as the means of passing information back to the main part of the CLIST.

9.3 Structure of Subprocedures
- A subprocedure begins with a label. (Alphanumeric string, beginning with a letter and ending with a colon).
- It must contain a PROC statement, which allows it to receive data passed from the caller on a SYSCALL.
- It must physically end with an END instruction, which is matched with the subprocedure definition.
- Flow of control ends with either one of the following:
- an END instruction (if there is no RETURN or EXIT)
- a RETURN instruction, which can pass a number (a return code) back
- END is the logical delimiter of your subprocedure, and is also the instruction that terminates it, if you don't terminate it first with a RETURN or EXIT.
- END can be changed to something else, with a CONTROL END
- Your subprocedure may not be the first thing in your program, or the CLIST interpreter will take its PROC statement as the PROC statement for the entire CLIST.
- Subprocedures may be anywhere else in the program, but the logical place for them is at the physical end of the program.
- You do not *need* an EXIT instruction before your subprocedures, because control will not fall through to a subprocedure. Good programming practice dictates that all your subprocedures are placed all together at the physical end of your program, clearly delimited by adequate comments.
- Last, subprocedures are contained physically in the CLIST program that references them. There are no *external* subprocedures.

Chapter 9: Writing Subprocedures

Purpose of REXX Subroutines

- CLIST subprocedures and REXX subroutines are used for the same purposes.

Capabilities of Subroutines

- REXX subroutines can receive input parameters (strings of data or variables), or can be executed without input parameters.
- Subroutines can execute REXX instructions and/or TSO commands.
- Subroutines can pass a number (a return code) back to the instruction after the one that invoked them, or they can return control without a number.
- They can pass information (a number or a character string, generally the result of the subprocedure's processing) back to the main part of the program on the RETURN instruction.

Structure of Subroutines

- A subroutine begins with a label, as for CLIST.
- It may contain an ARG or PARSE ARG instruction, which allows it to receive data passed from the caller on a CALL. (Note: there is a REXX PROCEDURE instruction, but it is nowhere near the same as CLIST PROC. It *hides* variables from the main part of the program.)
- There is no specific physical delimiter for subroutines. Indicate the physical end by means of comments.
- RETURN is the logical delimiter for subroutines. A RETURN terminates the subroutine's execution. (An EXIT will terminate it too, and also terminate the main program.)
- Your subroutine should be at the physical end of your program. The flow of control will drop into subroutines unless you have an EXIT before the first subroutine.
- Last, subroutines are contained physically in the REXX program that references them. There are no *external* subroutines. There are external and internal REXX functions, which are beyond the scope of this book.

9.4 Examples of Subprocedures

The simplest of the simple. This subprocedure just does something. It might be allocating a dataset (the same one each time it's executed) checking on the time (as in this example) or anything else that doesn't require a change of input, or the result of some process or calculation.

No variables are shared with the main part of the program.

```
/* CLST0045  SIMPLE SUBPROCEDURE. JUST DO SOMETHING */
WRITE IN MAIN PART OF CLIST
SET SALARY = 1000
SYSCALL MYSUB /* CALLING THE SUBPROCEDURE */
WRITE AFTER CALLING THE SUBPROCEDURE
WRITE ILLUSTRATING THAT THE VARIABLE DEPARTMENT IS NOT SHARED:
WRITE &DEPARTMENT
EXIT /* LOGICAL END OF PROGRAM (NOT REQUIRED) */


MYSUB: PROC 0  /* start of the subprocedure */
   WRITE CONTROL IS IN THE SUBPROCEDURE
   WRITE &SYSDATE &SYSTIME
   WRITE ILLUSTRATING THAT THE VARIABLE SALARY IS NOT SHARED:
   WRITE &SALARY
   SET DEPARTMENT = 2D1
END /* LOGICAL/physical END OF THE SUBP. RETURNS CONTROL */
```

A more typical subprocedure. Something is passed to it (a dataset name in this example), it does something with the dataset name, and then passes a number back indicating whether the command succeeded or failed. This subprocedure does not have the ability to pass back any information other than the number on the RETURN instruction.

No variables are shared with the main part of the program.

```
/* CLST0046  SUBPROCEDURE. PASS DATA TO IT                 */
/* SUBPROCEDURE RETURNS CODE INDICATING SUCCESS OR FAILURE */
WRITE IN MAIN PART OF CLIST
SET DSN = MYLIB.DATA.CLIST
SYSCALL MYSUB &DSN /* CALLING THE SUBPROCEDURE, PASSING &DSN */
WRITE RETURN CODE FROM SUBPROCEDURE WAS &LASTCC
EXIT  /* LOGICAL END OF PROGRAM (NOT REQUIRED) */


MYSUB: PROC 1 DATASET_PASSED_TO_PROCEDURE
   CONTROL LIST NOFLUSH
   WRITE SUBPROCEDURE RECEIVED &DATASET_PASSED_TO_PROCEDURE
   ALLOCATE DDN(TEMP001) SHR REUSE DSN(&DATASET_PASSED_TO_PROCEDURE)
   SET HOLD_CC = &LASTCC
   WRITE &HOLD_CC WAS RETURN CODE FROM ALLOCATE
   RETURN CODE(&HOLD_CC) /* RETURNS CONTROL AND PASSES NUMBER BACK */
END /* LOGICAL END OF THE SUBPROCEDURE. */
```

Examples of REXX Subroutines

The simplest of the simple. This subroutine just does something. It might be allocating a dataset (the same one each time it's executed) checking on the time (as in this example) or anything else that doesn't require a change of input, or the result of some process or calculation.

Variables are shared, by default, with the main part of the program.

```
/* REXX0045  SIMPLE SUBROUTINE. JUST DO SOMETHING */
SAY "IN MAIN PART OF PROGRAM "
SALARY = 1000
CALL MYSUB /* CALLING THE SUBROUTINE */
SAY "AFTER CALLING THE SUBROUTINE"
SAY "ILLUSTRATING THAT THE VARIABLE DEPARTMENT IS SHARED:"
SAY DEPARTMENT
EXIT /* LOGICAL END OF PROGRAM (REQUIRED) */

MYSUB:         /* START OF THE SUBROUTINE */
   SAY "CONTROL IS IN THE SUBROUTINE"
   SAY DATE(U) TIME()
   SAY "ILLUSTRATING THAT THE VARIABLE SALARY IS SHARED:"
   SAY SALARY
   DEPARTMENT = "2D1"
RETURN /* LOGICAL END OF THE SUBROUTINE. RETURNS CONTROL */
```

A more typical subroutine. Something is passed to it (a dataset name in this example), it does something with the dataset name, and then passes a number back indicating whether the command succeeded or failed. This subroutine could have passed back a character string, as well as the number on the RETURN instruction. Variables are shared, by default, with the main part of the program.

```
/* REXX0046  SUBROUTINE. PASS DATA TO IT                 */
/* SUBROUTINE RETURNS CODE INDICATING SUCCESS OR FAILURE */
SAY "IN MAIN PART OF PROGRAM"
DSN = "MYLIB.DATA.CLIST"
CALL MYSUB DSN /* CALLING THE SUBROUTINE, PASSING DSN */
SAY "RETURN CODE FROM SUBROUTINE WAS" RESULT
EXIT  /* LOGICAL END OF PROGRAM (REQUIRED) */

MYSUB: ARG DATASET_PASSED_TO_PROCEDURE
   SAY "SUBROUTINE RECEIVED" DATASET_PASSED_TO_PROCEDURE
   "ALLOCATE DDN(TEMP001) SHR REUSE DSN("DATASET_PASSED_TO_PROCEDURE")"
   HOLD_CC = RC
   SAY HOLD_CC "WAS RETURN CODE FROM ALLOCATE "
   RETURN HOLD_CC /* RETURNS CONTROL AND PASSES NUMBER BACK */
```

An even more useful subprocedure. Information is passed to it; it performs a calculation; it passes back the result of the calculation using SYSREF. Since variables are not shared with the main part of the CLIST, you must designate one or more variables as the means by which you pass back information. (This is one of the most confusing aspects of CLISTs.)

The line numbers are not part of the executable program. They are for reference only.

Line 5: You must give a value to the variable that will receive data passed back by the subprocedure. This significant fact is not mentioned in the vendor manuals.

Line 6: Calling the subprocedure. There are three data items on the call: &SALARY &MULTIPLY_BY and RETURNED_DATA. &SALARY and &MULTIPLY_BY are variables whose values you are passing *to* the subprocedure. RETURNED_DATA is the variable which will be *set by* the subprocedure. Its current value is irrelevant, but it must have a value.

Line 10: The definition of the subprocedure. It must be a name followed by a colon. Since you are passing data, you must have a PROC statement with a number that counts the items on it, 3 in this example.

The names of the data items are different from, but similar to, those in the main part of the CLIST. (They can be the same, but that would only add to the possible confusion.)

The first two data items in this example are *receiving* data; the third is going to *pass back* data. There is nothing on the PROC statement that tells you that.

Line 11: The SYSREF instruction specifies the variable RET_DATA that is also on the PROC instruction. SYSREF means that this variable is the pipeline by which you will pass data back to the main part of the program. It's actually referring to the variable RETURNED_DATA

Line 14: The subprocedure sets the variable RET_DATA to the result of the calculation. RET_DATA is not passed back to the main part of the program: RET_DATA replaces RETURNED_DATA!

Line 6 again: The third item on the call is the variable that will be changed by the subprocedure. It does not have an ampersand, since you don't want its value; you want its name.

Line 7: The variable &RETURNED_DATA now has the result of the calculation in the subprocedure.

```
01 /* CLST0047  SUBPROCEDURE. PASS DATA TO IT                */
02 /* SUBPROCEDURE PASSES BACK THE RESULT OF A CALCULATION   */
03 SET SALARY        = 1000
04 SET MULTIPLY_BY   = 10
05 SET RETURNED_DATA = 0 /* MUST HAVE A VALUE! */
06 SYSCALL MYSUB &SALARY &MULTIPLY_BY RETURNED_DATA
07 WRITE SUBPROCEDURE CALCULATED NEW SALARY AS &RETURNED_DATA
08 EXIT  /* LOGICAL END OF PROGRAM (NOT REQUIRED) */
09
10 MYSUB: PROC 3 SAL MULT RET_DATA
11    SYSREF RET_DATA
12    WRITE IN SUBPROCEDURE: RECEIVED &SAL AND &MULT
13    SET RET_DATA = &SAL * &MULT
14    WRITE IN SUBPROCEDURE: CALCULATED &RET_DATA
15 END /* LOGICAL END OF THE SUBPROCEDURE. RETURNS CONTROL */
```

An even more useful subroutine in REXX. Information is passed to it; it performs a calculation; it passes back the result of the calculation on its RETURN. The main part of the program sees the answer in the reserved variable RESULT.

The line numbers are not part of the executable program. They are for reference only.

Line 5: Calling the subroutine. There are two variables on the call: SALARY and MULTIPLY_BY, whose values you are passing *to* the subroutine.

Line 9: The definition of the subroutine. It must be a name followed by a colon. Since you are passing data, you must have an ARG (or PARSE ARG) statement with variables on it. (I normally use commas here, on the ARG and on the CALL, but don't here, to make it more like the CLIST. Both ways work.)

Line 11. The subroutine sets the variable RET_DATA with the result of the calculation.

Line 13. The RETURN instruction passes back the contents of RET_DATA to the main part of the program, which receives it in the reserved variable RESULT.

```
1 /* REXX0047  SUBROUTINE. PASS DATA TO IT                 */
2 /* SUBROUTINE PASSES BACK THE RESULT OF A CALCULATION    */
3 SALARY        = 1000
4 MULTIPLY_BY   = 10
5 CALL MYSUB SALARY MULTIPLY_BY
6 SAY "SUBROUTINE CALCULATED NEW SALARY AS" RESULT
7 EXIT  /* LOGICAL END OF PROGRAM (REQUIRED) */
8
9  MYSUB: ARG SAL MULT
10     SAY "IN SUBROUTINE: RECEIVED" SAL "AND" MULT
11     RET_DATA = SAL * MULT
12     SAY "IN SUBROUTINE: CALCULATED" RET_DATA
13 RETURN RET_DATA /* LOGICAL END OF SUB. RETURNS CONTROL */
```

A simpler way to pass information back from the subprocedure.
The preceding method, with SYSREF, can be confusing. By using NGLOBAL you can share one or more variables.
This allows you to specify one or more variables that are in the subprocedure as shared with the main part of the program and among all subprocedures in your CLIST program. This is much simpler and easier to understand than SYSREF. The vendor manual does not tell you that this shares variables with the main part of the program.
If you want the variable SYSTEMID to be shared among all your subprocedures in your program, you code NGLOBAL SYSTEMID in each of your subprocedures. This makes the variable SYSTEMID available to the main part of the program, and in each of your subprocedures that also has coded NGLOBAL SYSTEMID
Placing NGLOBAL in the main part of your CLIST does nothing. It must be in one or more subprocedures.
In the following example, the variable RET_DATA is defined on a NGLOBAL statement in the subprocedure. That makes it shared with the rest of the CLIST program, as well as any other subprocedures.

```
/* CLST0048  SUBPROCEDURE. PASS DATA TO IT                 */
/* SUBPROCEDURE SHARES ONE VARIABLE WITH MAIN PART OF CLIST  */
/* USING NGLOBAL                                           */
SET SALARY       = 1000
SET MULTIPLY_BY  = 15
SYSCALL MYSUB &SALARY &MULTIPLY_BY
WRITE SUBPROCEDURE CALCULATED NEW SALARY AS &RET_DATA
EXIT  /* LOGICAL END OF PROGRAM (NOT REQUIRED) */

MYSUB: PROC 2 SAL MULT
   NGLOBAL RET_DATA
   WRITE IN SUBPROCEDURE: RECEIVED &SAL AND &MULT
   SET RET_DATA = &SAL * &MULT
   WRITE IN SUBPROCEDURE: CALCULATED &RET_DATA
END /* LOGICAL END OF THE SUBPROCEDURE. RETURNS CONTROL */
```

There is no need for a simpler way to pass information back in REXX
RETURN plus a character string, a number, or a variable sends information back to the caller, which can pick it up in the reserved variable RESULT.

9.5 Reference for the syntax of PROC statement in subprocedures, ARG in REXX Subroutines and Functions.

CLIST PROC

- The PROC statement is required, at the beginning of a subprocedure, even if there are no parameters and you code PROC 0.
- Values passed will be converted to uppercase, unless a CONTROL CAPS or CONTROL ASIS is in effect.
- It may have positional parameters, which you must count; you put the count on the PROC statement.
- It may have keyword parameters as well. Keyword parameters may have a default value, or empty parentheses.
- There is no prompting for missing parameters on the SYSCALL. Omitting one or more causes an error exception.
- Your SYSCALL instruction must specify a value for each of the positional parameters. The values may be in variables; none of the variables may be blank, contain blanks, or have zero characters.
- Do not separate the values with commas. They are ignored on the SYSCALL and on the PROC.

REXX ARG in Subroutines

- REXX ARG is an abbreviation of PARSE UPPER ARG.
- ARG and PARSE UPPER ARG are the nearest equivalents to CLIST PROC.
- A REXX subroutine doesn't *have* to have an ARG. Variables are shared by default with the main part of the program.
- If you don't want the data converted to uppercase, code PARSE ARG instead.
- ARG has positional parameters, just like CLIST PROC.
- ARG does not have keyword parameters.
- There is no prompting for missing parameters on the CALL.
- A missing value causes the corresponding variable to be set to 0 characters.
- The CALL may pass literal strings, preferably bounded by quotes or apostrophes, or variables.
- A literal string or a variable may be blank or contain 0 characters.
- Literal strings bounded by quotes or apostrophes may contain blanks.
- You may want to use spaces instead of commas between the parameters. This will make your REXX subroutine more like your CLIST subprocedure.
  ```
  CALL MYSUB "JOE" "2325656" "48 Pine St"
  ```
  in the subroutine:
  ```
  ARG NAME PHONE ADDR
  ```
- It works *with* commas or *without* commas. Consistency is the key.
- You do not have to pass values to a subroutine, unless the subroutine requires them. In that case the subroutine will have to check for them.
- If the CALL has more values than the ARG has variables, the additional values are put into the last variable.
- If the CALL has fewer values than the ARG has variables, the leftmost variable(s) are set to null.

This page intentionally left blank

Chapter 10: Interacting with the User

Chapter 10 is about the way your CLIST gets data from the user, and how it displays it.

Chapter 10 contains:

Chapter 10: Interacting with the User

10.1 PROC

- Your CLIST may have a PROC statement. If it does, then information can be passed to the CLIST when it is executed, on the command line.
- It must be the first executable statement in the program, if present.

Starting with an example:

```
PROC 3 NAME ADDR PHONE    STATE(NY) WEEKDAY(MONDAY) CALENDAR(GREGORIAN)
```

There are three positional (required) parameters on the PROC statement: NAME ADDR PHONE. You must count them and put the number on the PROC statement. 3 in this example.

- `WEEKDAY(MONDAY)` `CALENDAR(GREGORIAN)` are keyword (optional) parameters. You may change their value at execution time, or you may let them default to the value already specified.
- When executing the CLIST, you must enter all three positional parameters, or TSO will ask you for them.
- You must enter a non-space character. Some characters are not accepted, such as "["
- You must enter them in the right order–that's why they are called "positional parameters."
- The parameters after the first 3, in this example, are "keyword parameters", and they have a default value, so they don't have to be entered.
- If you enter one or more of the keyword parameters, that value will override the default value.
- If you don't enter one or more of them, the default values will be used.
- They must come after the positionals, both on the PROC and on the command line during execution.
- In the example just below, STATE is changed to "PA".
- If you enter too many words, it is an error and your CLIST is not executed.

At execution time:
```
==> clst0060 john 148a 2125554583 state(pa)
```

Upon execution, all of the CLIST variables will be set.

      NAME will equal "JOHN"
      ADDR will equal "148A"
      PHONE will equal "2125554583"
      STATE will equal "PA"
      WEEKDAY will equal "MONDAY"
      CALENDAR will equal "GREGORIAN"

All data is uppercased. All the variables named on the PROC are set to something.

See the example of a CLIST with a PROC statement, on the next left-hand page.

<u>INITIAL ARG, PARSE ARG</u>
REXX ARG is the nearest equivalent to CLIST PROC. It works very differently, however.

The differences:
- ARG can be at the beginning of a REXX program, or it can be in a subroutine or function. The one that corresponds to the initial CLIST PROC must be at the beginning of your REXX program. (I know that it can be *anywhere*, but it makes no sense to put it any place other than at the beginning.)
- All parameters are positional.
- You don't count the parameters as you do on a PROC.
- There are no keyword parameters.
- TSO will not ask you for missing parameters.
- If you enter only 1 word, the first variable is set and the others are set to null. If you enter 2, the first two variables are set and the others are set to null. Same for 3.
- If you enter too many words, the excess words are contained in the last variable, along with the expected information.
- There are big differences in how they handle delimiters in the data entered.
  You are entering words, and there cannot be spaces in a word. Putting values in quotes doesn't work. Convert, then test a lot.
- You cannot use a leading comma to indicate a missing parameter.
- When executing REXX, commas on the command line cause trouble. Do not separate the values with commas. Commas do not have any special meaning on the command line. Separate the parameters with spaces.
- Data is not uppercased, if you use PARSE ARG. It is uppercased if you use ARG.

Example of a CLIST with a PROC statement

Here is a short CLIST, written for illustration purposes. It collects and displays the positional and keyword parameters.

```
/* CLST0049 TO ILLUSTRATE PROC STATEMENT */
PROC 3 NAME ADDR PHONE   STATE(NY) WEEKDAY(MONDAY) CALENDAR(GREGORIAN)
WRITE &STR(POSITIONAL PARAMETERS AS RESOLVED)
WRITE &STR(NAME) &NAME
WRITE &STR(ADDR) &ADDR
WRITE &STR(PHONE) &PHONE
WRITE &STR(KEYWORD   PARAMETERS AS RESOLVED)
WRITE &STR(STATE) &STATE
WRITE &STR(WEEKDAY) &WEEKDAY
WRITE &STR(CALENDAR) &CALENDAR
```

Here are the results with various methods of execution:
Command line:

```
==> clst0049 joe 22Elm 2025552121
```

Results displayed:

```
POSITIONAL PARAMETERS AS RESOLVED
NAME JOE
ADDR 22ELM
PHONE 2025552121
KEYWORD   PARAMETERS AS RESOLVED
STATE NY
WEEKDAY MONDAY
CALENDAR GREGORIAN


==> clst0049 joe 22Elm
ENTER POSITIONAL PARAMETER PHONE -
4055553234

POSITIONAL PARAMETERS AS RESOLVED
NAME JOE
ADDR 22ELM
PHONE 4055553234
KEYWORD   PARAMETERS AS RESOLVED
STATE NY
WEEKDAY MONDAY
CALENDAR GREGORIAN


==> clst0049 joe 22Elm 7764544545 state(ca)
POSITIONAL PARAMETERS AS RESOLVED
NAME JOE
ADDR 22ELM
PHONE 7764544545
KEYWORD   PARAMETERS AS RESOLVED
STATE CA
WEEKDAY MONDAY
CALENDAR GREGORIAN
```

Example

Writing a REXX program that simulates the action of CLIST PROC can take a long time. I created a program that does just that. You will find it on my website along with the other named CLISTs and REXX programs. You can find it printed and explained in this book, in Supplement 3.

10.2 WRITE

WRITE displays information on the terminal. It resolves variables but does not do arithmetic.

```
SET NAME = GEORGE
WRITE EMPLOYEE &NAME WILL RECEIVE 1000 * 2 DOLLAR BONUS
```

Displays:

```
EMPLOYEE GEORGE WILL RECEIVE 1000 * 2 DOLLAR BONUS
```

To do arithmetic, use the &EVAL function:

```
SET NAME = GEORGE
WRITE EMPLOYEE &NAME WILL RECEIVE &EVAL(1000 * 2) DOLLAR BONUS
```

Displays:

```
EMPLOYEE GEORGE WILL RECEIVE 2000 DOLLAR BONUS
```

10.3 WRITENR

This is the same as WRITE, except that the cursor remains at the rightmost end of the line. This is used when the CLIST asks for information and expects it to be typed in. It makes the request more obvious than dropping the cursor down to the next line.

```
WRITENR PLEASE ENTER MULTIPLIER FOR BONUS
READ MULTIPLIER
SET BONUS = 1000 * &MULTIPLIER
WRITE THE BONUS IS &BONUS
```

Results:

```
PLEASE ENTER MULTIPLIER FOR BONUS  33
THE BONUS IS 33000
```

WRITE equivalent in REXX

SAY displays information at the terminal. You use it for messages and to ask for input. It resolves variables and does arithmetic.

```
NAME = "GEORGE"
SAY "EMPLOYEE" NAME "WILL RECEIVE" 1000 * 2 "DOLLAR BONUS"
```
Displays:
```
EMPLOYEE GEORGE WILL RECEIVE 2000 DOLLAR BONUS
```

To prevent arithmetic, or variable substitution, enclose everything in quotes.
```
NAME = "GEORGE"
SAY "EMPLOYEE NAME WILL RECEIVE 1000 * 2 DOLLAR BONUS"
```
Displays:
```
EMPLOYEE NAME WILL RECEIVE 1000 * 2 DOLLAR BONUS
```

WRITENR

There is no REXX equivalent for WRITENR.

10.4 READ

READ accepts input typed at the terminal. A WRITE or WRITENR is done before the READ to tell the user what to type in.

READ normally specifies one or more variables. They all will be changed during the execution of the READ statement.

```
WRITE PLEASE ENTER NAME ADDRESS PHONE
READ NAME ADDRESS PHONE
WRITE THANK YOU &NAME &ADDRESS &PHONE
```

Data entered is taken as words, delimited by one or more spaces. (Leading and trailing spaces are ignored.)
If you want to include spaces in a value entered, enter it bounded by apostrophes:
`'27 Brightwood Road'`   The apostrophes are dropped.
This fact has made it difficult to write CLISTs that handle TSO dataset names according to TSO naming standards. You DO NOT want the user to type in three consecutive apostrophes when only one is actually needed, around a TSO dataset name. (But it works.)
This leads to workarounds that force the user to enter a dataset name contrary to standard naming conventions. (See below in this book, Supplement 1, Specifying Dataset Names in TSO Commands.)

Commas may be used to indicate omitted words:
`,,2125554848`   The first two words are entered as blanks.

READ does not prompt for missing data.
A READ without variables causes the data entered to go into &SYSDVAL
Data in &SYSDVAL can be broken apart into words using READDVAL. (See the next entry.)

READ substitute: REXX PULL

PULL can accomplish the same thing as CLIST READ. It uses the stack, or Internal Data Queue, for which there is no equivalent in CLIST. If your REXX program is not using the stack/Internal Data Queue, PULL is close to CLIST READ.

You specify one or more variables on the PULL instruction. They will all be changed during the execution of the pull instruction.

```
SAY "PLEASE ENTER NAME ADDRESS PHONE"
PULL NAME ADDRESS PHONE
SAY "THANK YOU" NAME ADDRESS PHONE
```

Data entered is taken as words, delimited by one or more spaces. (Leading and trailing spaces are ignored.)

PULL is actually a form of the REXX PARSE verb which has many variations and options that CLIST READ does not have.

PULL does not prompt for missing data.

Commas do not function the same way at all with REXX. If your ARG has commas between the variables, you must use commas to separate the items of data that you enter. If your ARG has no commas, then entering data with commas will not work right. (To put it very briefly, a comma would indicate the end of the data entered.)

Entering a dataset name is not a problem. What you type in is what is accepted. If you enter a dataset name according to standard TSO naming conventions, it is accepted and treated as such.

10.5 READDVAL

A READ with no variables puts the information in &SYSDVAL

```
    WRITE PLEASE ENTER YOUR NAME
READ /* no operands*/
WRITE &SYSDVAL /* returns whatever the user typed in,*/
               /* without change */
```

Putting a string of data in &SYSDVAL allows you to use the READDVAL instruction to break up the data into several variables.

```
/* CLST0007 TO ILLUSTRATE &SYSDVAL AND READDVAL
SET SYSDVAL = A STRING OF DATA
READDVAL VAR1 VAR2 VAR3 VAR4 VAR5
WRITE &VAR1
WRITE &VAR2
WRITE &VAR3
WRITE &VAR4
WRITE &VAR5 /* IN THIS EXAMPLE, &VAR5 WILL BE NULL */
```

Commas may be used to indicate omitted words as for READ:
```
,,2125554848
```
The first two words are entered as blanks.

10.6 TERMIN

It's unlikely that any surviving CLIST has a functional TERMIN statement in it. TERMIN does not work under ISPF, or under the Session Manager or in a batch job run through JCL.

READDVAL Substitute in REXX
The nearest equivalent for CLIST READDVAL is REXX PARSE.

```
/* REXX PROGRAM REXX0007 BREAKING UP DATA INTO WORDS. */
SIMULATE_SYSDVAL = "A STRING OF DATA"
PARSE UPPER VAR SIMULATE_SYSDVAL VAR1 VAR2 VAR3 VAR4 VAR5
/* IN THIS EXAMPLE, VAR5 WILL BE NULL */
SAY VAR1
SAY VAR2
SAY VAR3
SAY VAR4
SAY VAR5
```

TERMIN
No equivalent to this in REXX.

Chapter 10: Interacting with the User

This page intentionally left blank

Chapter 11: Executing TSO Commands

Chapter 11 is about the main reason why CLISTs exist: to execute TSO commands and/or subcommands. If you need additional information about TSO commands, see Supplement 1 in this book.

Chapter 11 contains:

Chapter 11: Executing TSO Commands

11.1 Overview

CLIST means Command List. The CLIST language was devised to allow more control over the execution of TSO Line Mode (Native Mode, or Ready Mode) commands and/or subcommands. CLIST allows you to introduce variability into the execution of commands. With CLIST you can verify information entered, before actually executing a command based on the information. By examining &LASTCC or &MAXCC you can determine if a command or subcommand worked, and display information to the user, or sometimes take corrective action.

TSO commands include the following:

ALLOCATE	to link to a file
FREE	to release the link to a file
CALL	to execute a compiled program
DELETE	to delete a dataset
EDIT	to enter into the Line Mode Editor
SUBMIT	to send JCL to the batch system for processing.

(For a tutorial on TSO Line Mode commands, see Supplement 1 in this book).

The command or subcommand may be specified in uppercase or lowercase. TSO converts the command to uppercase.

To make a command go to ISPF, put the word ISPEXEC in front of it:

```
ISPEXEC VGET VAR1
```

To make a command go to the ISPF editor, put the word ISREDIT in front of it, for example:

```
ISREDIT FIND FIRST ABC
```

Chapter 11: Executing TSO Commands

Overview

REXX and CLIST both excel at passing commands to the operating system in which they execute. The major difference with REXX, is that REXX gives you the return code from the command in the reserved variable RC.

Anything that is first on the line, and that is in quotes, will be passed by REXX to TSO. Any unrecognized character string that is first on the line, and that is not an assignment, will be passed by REXX to TSO.

Commands are sent to TSO by default.

To make a command go to ISPF, you can do one of two things:
> put the word ISPEXEC in front of it, for example:
> **`"ISPEXEC VGET VAR1"`**
> or
> use the ADDRESS instruction:
> **`ADDRESS ISPEXEC "VGET VAR1"`**

To make a command go to the ISPF editor, you can do one of two things:
> put the word ISREDIT in front of it, for example:
> **`"ISREDIT FIND FIRST ABC"`**
> or
> use the ADDRESS instruction:
> **`ADDRESS ISREDIT "FIND FIRST ABC"`**

You never need to prefix a TSO command with ADDRESS TSO, unless you have previously done ADDRESS ISPEXEC or ADDRESS ISREDIT *on a separate line by itself*. (That changes the default for the currently running program.)

11.2 How to Specify TSO Commands
Simplest mode.
You may enter the command into the CLIST exactly as it would be typed in at the terminal, in "Ready Mode," outside of ISPF (or under TSO/ISPF, in Option 6). No delimiters or special considerations are needed.

For example:
```
DELETE ABC.DATA
```

Note that under TSO/ISPF, in any screen except Option 6, you must prefix the TSO command with the word TSO:
```
TSO DELETE ABC.DATA
```
You do not prefix commands with "TSO" in a CLIST.

Long commands may be continued with a continuation character (+ or -).
```
DELETE (ABD.DATA CDE.DATA DEF.DATA +
   XYZ.DATA YZZ.DATA)
```

Command with a variable
Commands passed to TSO may be specified with variables. The variable is resolved before the command is passed to TSO.
```
SET DSN = MYDATA.DATA
DELETE &DSN
```

```
SET R = REUSE
 CONTROL LIST
 ALLOCATE DDNAME(TEMP) SPACE(1) NEW DELETE TRACKS &R
```

Command with arithmetic operator
Arithmetic operations specified on a command will *not* be performed before the command is passed to TSO. To have the arithmetic done, enclose the operation in &EVAL.
```
ALLOC DDN(TEMP) SPACE(&EVAL(1 + 1)) NEW DELETE TRACKS REUSE
```

11.3 Return Codes
If a TSO command fails or doesn't work properly, it gives back a non-zero return code which you can examine in &LASTCC. If you need to use it later, save it in a variable, since every instruction or command sets &LASTCC too. &MAXCC contains the highest &LASTCC returned, to date, during execution of your CLIST.

Chapter 11: Executing TSO Commands

How to Specify TSO Commands in REXX
Simplest mode.
The command should be enclosed in quotes. Quotes, not apostrophes, because some TSO commands use apostrophes (SEND, ALLOCATE, FREE, DELETE and others.)

Enter the command into the REXX program exactly as it would be typed in at the terminal, in "Ready Mode," outside of ISPF (or under TSO/ISPF, in Option 6), with quotes around it.

For example:
```
"DELETE ABC.DATA"
```

Note that under TSO/ISPF, in any screen except Option 6, you must prefix the TSO command with the word TSO:
```
TSO DELETE ABC.DATA
```
You do not prefix commands with "TSO" in a REXX program. (ADDRESS TSO is another matter entirely. It has nothing to do with this.)

Long commands may be continued with a comma.
```
"DELETE (ABD.DATA CDE.DATA DEF.DATA" ,
   "XYZ.DATA YZZ.DATA) "
```

Command with a variable in REXX
Commands passed to TSO may be specified with variables. The variable is outside of the quotes. The variable is resolved before the command is passed to TSO.
```
DSN = "MYDATA.DATA"
"DELETE" DSN
```

If you want apostrophes around the dataset name, enclose them in the quotes.
```
DSN = "'userid.MYDATA.DATA'"
"DELETE" DSN
```

```
R = REUSE
TRACE C
"ALLOCATE DDNAME(TEMP) SPACE(1) NEW DELETE TRACKS" R
```

Command with arithmetic operator
Arithmetic operations specified outside of quotes on a command will be performed before the command is passed to TSO.
```
"ALLOC DDN(TEMP) SPACE("1 + 1") NEW DELETE TRACKS REUSE "
```
To prevent the arithmetic, enclose the operation in quotes.

Note that this can lead to a line of code that is confusing at first glance.

Return Codes
If a TSO command fails or doesn't work properly, it gives back a non-zero return code which you can examine in RC. If you need to use it later, save it in a variable, since every TSO command sets RC too.

11.4 Sending Commands to ISPF

Most TSO work is done under ISPF. ISPF executes as a program under TSO. TSO executes under the main operating system, z/OS. If you are on ISPF you can send commands to ISPF. If you are in the ISPF Editor, you can send subcommands to the Editor. (The program that does that is an ISPF Editor macro.) ISPF and ISPF Editor subcommands are beyond the scope of this book.

Before you send a command to ISPF you need to know if you are actually executing under ISPF. You can use the control variable &SYSISPF. If ISPF is not active, you are in "Line Mode TSO" (Ready Mode, or Native Mode).

You should not have to find out if the ISPF Editor is available to your program because a program containing Editor subcommands can be executed successfully only while in the Editor, as a macro.

```
IF &SYSISPF = ACTIVE THEN WRITE OK TO SEND COMMANDS TO ISPF.
```

Examples of ISPF commands are:

VGET	retrieve variables
VPUT	store variables
SETMSG	display message on screen
SELECT	execute program
CONTROL	ISPF command that affects error situations

Examples of ISPF Editor commands are:

MACRO	declare that the program is a macro
CHANGE	change data
FIND	locate character strings
CAPS ON	convert data typed in to uppercase

Commands for ISPF are prefixed with "ISPEXEC".
Commands for the ISPF Editor are prefixed with "ISREDIT".

Example of a short program that uses ISPF Variable Services.
```
/* CLST0050 TO ILLUSTRATE AN ISPF COMMAND */
IF &SYSISPF = ACTIVE THEN +
ISPEXEC VGET SAVEDVAR
WRITE &SAVEDVAR /* NOTHING WAS SET, SO VARIABLE IS NULL */
```

Example of a short ISPF Editor macro:
Note: you execute it from the command line of your Editor session and you don't prefix it with "TSO".
```
===> %CLST0051
/* CLST0051 TO ILLUSTRATE A SHORT ISPF EDITOR MACRO */
ISREDIT MACRO            /* MUST BE FIRST THING IN THE PROGRAM */
ISREDIT FIND FIRST A     /* A SIMPLE EDITOR COMMAND */
```

Chapter 11: Executing TSO Commands

Sending Commands to ISPF with REXX

Most TSO work is done under ISPF. ISPF executes as a program under TSO. TSO executes under the main operating system, z/OS. If you are on ISPF you can send commands to ISPF. If you are in the ISPF Editor, you can send commands to the Editor. (The program that does that is an ISPF Editor macro.)
ISPF and ISPF Editor subcommands are beyond the scope of this book.

Before you send a command to ISPF you need to know if you are actually executing under ISPF. You can use SYSVAR("SYSISPF"). If ISPF is not active, you are in "Line Mode TSO" (Ready Mode, or Native Mode).

You should not have to find out if the ISPF Editor is available to your program because a program containing Editor subcommands can be executed successfully only while in the Editor, as a macro.

```
IF SYSVAR("SYSISPF") = "ACTIVE" THEN SAY "OK TO SEND COMMANDS TO ISPF"
```

Commands for ISPF are prefixed with "ISPEXEC". (There are other ways, but I'm showing you this way because it's closest to the CLIST way.)
Commands for the ISPF Editor are prefixed with "ISREDIT". (There are other ways, but I'm showing you this way because it's closest to the CLIST way.)

Example of a short program that uses ISPF Variable Services.
```
/* REXX0050 TO ILLUSTRATE AN ISPF COMMAND */
IF SYSVAR("SYSISPF") = "ACTIVE"
THEN "ISPEXEC VGET SAVEDVAR"
SAY SAVEDVAR /* NOTHING WAS SET, SO VARIABLE IS NULL */
```

Example of a short ISPF Editor macro:
Note: you execute it from the command line of your Editor session and you don't prefix it with "TSO".
```
===> %rexx0051
/* REXX0051 TO ILLUSTRATE A SHORT ISPF EDITOR MACRO */
"ISREDIT MACRO"              /* MUST BE FIRST THING IN THE PROGRAM */
"ISREDIT FIND FIRST A"       /* A SIMPLE EDITOR COMMAND */
```

This page intentionally left blank

Chapter 12: File IO

Chapter 12 is how you read or write records in QSAM datasets ("flat files," "sequential files") or PDS/PDSE members.

Chapter 12 contains:

Chapter 12: File IO

12.1 The Basics

You can read or write QSAM files ("flat files," "sequential files") with CLIST language. PDS/PDSE members may be used as input or output, but it is not possible to have two members open for output in the same PDS/PDSE at the same time.

- A TSO ALLOCATE command must be done first. It establishes a connection between a pointer to the file (a "DDNAME", a "file handle") and the actual file.
- If running your CLIST in batch, a JCL DD statement may be done instead.
- Open the file for INPUT, OUTPUT or UPDATE with the OPENFILE instruction.
- GETFILE reads a record
- PUTFILE writes a record
- Close the file. This is done with a CLOSFILE instruction.
- De-allocate (release) the file with the TSO FREE command.
  This breaks the connection between the file and the file pointer (the "DDNAME")

Closing the file at the end is essential. If you don't close it, you cannot de-allocate it with FREE. If you don't FREE it, you may prevent another TSO user or another job from accessing the file.

12.2 The ALLOCATE command for reading

If the ALLOCATE command doesn't work, your file IO will fail with numerous error messages. First, let's look at the ALLOCATE command used for reading.

```
ALLOC DDN(ddname) SHR REUSE DSN('dataset-you-are-reading')
```

Explanation of this command.
- ALLOC is the abbreviation of ALLOCATE.
- DDN is the abbreviation of DDNAME. This is equivalent to a JCL DD statement.
    An alternate form is F(ddname) or FILE(ddname).
    I suggest you use DDN, or DDNAME since this corresponds to the JCL parameter DDNAME.
- Do not use a DDNAME that TSO is already using for some other purpose. Use a name that doesn't start with SYS.
- SHR means that you don't mind if other users or jobs read this dataset at the same time as you.
- REUSE means that you will reassign or reuse this file pointer (DDNAME) if you have already used it since logging on to TSO. If not, no harm done.
- DSN is the actual dataset name you are trying to read. It must exist. You may also specify a PDS with member name in this form: MYLIB(MEMBER)
    An alternate form is DA('file-name-you-are-reading')
    I suggest you use DSN, since this corresponds to the JCL parameter DSNAME.

You may want to check the return code (&LASTCC) from the ALLOC command. If it is not zero, your file IO will fail with accusing error messages.

The Basics in REXX

CLIST IO and REXX IO are very similar. The major difference is that REXX can read an entire dataset into storage in one instruction. We are not going to show you that feature of REXX IO here. We will show you how to read one record at a time, just as you do with CLIST.

- A TSO ALLOCATE command must be done first. It establishes a connection between a pointer to the file (a "DDNAME", a "file handle") and the actual dataset.
- If running your REXX program in batch, a JCL DD statement may be done instead.
- DISKR on the instruction indicates that you are reading the file. It automatically opens the file for input, if it's not already open.
- DISKW on the instruction indicates that you are writing to the file. It automatically opens the file for output, if it's not already open.
- EXECIO 1 DISKR reads a record
- EXECIO 1 DISKW writes a record
- Close the file. This is done with the FINIS option on a EXECIO instruction.
- De-allocate (release) the dataset with the TSO FREE command.
  This breaks the connection between the dataset and the file pointer (the "DDNAME")

Closing the dataset at the end is essential. If you don't close it, you cannot de-allocate it with FREE. If you don't FREE it, you may prevent another TSO user or another job from accessing the dataset.

The ALLOCATE command for reading

The only difference in REXX is that the command is enclosed in quotes.

```
"ALLOC DDN(ddname) SHR REUSE DSN('dataset-you-are-reading')"
```

It is a good idea to check the return code (RC) from the ALLOC command. If it is not zero, your file IO will fail with accusing error messages.

12.3 Reading

After a successful ALLOCATE, and an OPENFILE INPUT, you can do a GETFILE.
GETFILE reads the entire record into a variable whose name is equal to the file handle (DDNAME).
In this example, the file handle (DDNAME) is INFILE.
When you reach the end of file, it is considered an error exception. An ERROR routine is needed to trap the error exception and allow you to close the file. The error exception for end of file is 400, but you might want to check for other exceptions as well, or the program may go into an unending loop.

```
/* CLST0052 EXAMPLE OF READING A FILE */
ALLOC DDN(INFILE) SHR REUSE DSN('dataset-you-are-reading')
    ERROR DO
        WRITE &LASTCC
        IF &LASTCC NE 0 THEN SET EOF = YES
        RETURN
    END

    SET EOF = NO

    OPENFILE INFILE INPUT
    DO UNTIL &EOF = YES
        GETFILE INFILE
        IF &EOF NE YES THEN DO
            WRITE RECORD READ WAS:
            WRITE &INFILE
        END /* EOF NE YES */
    END /* DO WHILE */

    CLOSFILE INFILE
    FREE DDNAME(INFILE)
```

The record is contained in a variable whose name is the same as the DDNAME.

Many things can go wrong when reading files. You may want to display &LASTCC after each command or instruction and use CONTROL LIST CONLIST, while testing.

Reading with REXX

After a successful ALLOCATE you can do an EXECIO DISKR ddname, where ddname is the file handle (DDNAME) that you used on the ALLOCATE. In this example, the file handle (DDNAME) is INFILE.

This example shows reading one record at a time with REXX, to make it as close to the CLIST example as possible. (REXX can read an entire file into a set of compound variables, or into the stack [Internal Data Queue].)

When you reach the end of file TSO gives you a 2 in the reserved variable RC. You need to examine this variable to determine when to end the loop that reads records.

```
/* REXX0052 EXAMPLE OF READING A FILE                 */
/* READS ONE RECORD AT A TIME INTO A STEM VARIABLE    */
/* ONLY THE FIRST ELEMENT OF THE STEM VARIABLE IS USED! */
/* TRACE C */
"ALLOC DDN(INFILE) SHR REUSE DSN('dataset-you-are-reading')"

EOF = "NO"

DO I = 1 WHILE EOF = "NO"
   "EXECIO 1 DISKR INFILE (STEM INFILE.)"
    IF RC <> 0 THEN DO
       EOF = "YES"
    END /* RC <> 0 */
    ELSE DO
       SAY "RECORD READ WAS "
       SAY INFILE.1
    END  /* RC  = 0 */
END /* DO WHILE */

"EXECIO 0 DISKR INFILE (FINIS)" /*CLOSE THE FILE */
"FREE DDNAME(INFILE)"
```

The record is contained in a variable whose name is what is specified on the STEM keyword, with a .1 appended: (INFILE.1). When doing things this way, there is only one variable, and it contains the record that was just read. You may use a different name, and it doesn't need to be the same as the DDNAME as I did in the example.

12.4 The ALLOCATE Command for Writing

If the ALLOCATE command doesn't work, your file IO will fail with numerous error messages. Let's look at the ALLOCATE command used with writing.

Three possibilities:

1. The dataset exists and you want to write over it:

```
ALLOC DDN(ddname) OLD REUSE DSN('dataset-to-write')
```

There is no difference between this ALLOC and the one used for reading, except for OLD. OLD means exclusive access, so no other job or user can read it while you are using it.

2. You need a dataset just like another:

```
ALLOC DDN(ddname) NEW REUSE DSN('dataset-to-write')   +
    LIKE('dataset-name-used-as-a-model')
```

The LIKE creates a new dataset just like another one. Everything is the same except the disk volume and the data contents. If the new dataset exists already, you should use the ALLOC shown in #1 just above, instead. If you don't know if it exists you may use this CLIST code:

```
      SET DSN = 'dataset-name-to-write'
      IF &SYSDSN(&DSN) = OK
      THEN +
      ALLOC DDN(ddname) OLD REUSE DSN(&DSN)
      ELSE +
      ALLOC DDN(ddname) NEW REUSE DSN(&DSN)   +
            LIKE ('dataset-name-used-as-a-model')
```

3. There is no model dataset. My advice is to allocate the dataset using TSO ISPF option 3.2 before running the program.

You can do the full ALLOCATE:

```
      ALLOC DDN(ddname) NEW REUSE DSN('dataset-to-write')   +
        LRECL(record-length) RECFM(F B) SPACE(10 10) TRACKS
```

It's a good idea to use the logic shown just above, with SYSDSN, like this:

```
      SET DSN = 'dataset-name-to-write'
      IF &SYSDSN(&DSN) = OK
      THEN +
      ALLOC DDN(ddname) OLD REUSE DSN(&DSN)
      ELSE
      ALLOC DDN(ddname) NEW REUSE DSN(&DSN)   +
      LRECL(record-length) RECFM(F B) SPACE(10 10) TRACKS
```

See the examples of writing to a dataset on the next left-hand page.

The ALLOCATE Command for Writing for REXX

The logic for REXX is the same as for CLIST. The format of the TSO commands is different.

Three possibilities:
1. The file exists and you want to write over it:

```
"ALLOC DDN(ddname) OLD REUSE DSN('dataset-to-write') "
```

There is no difference between this ALLOC and the one used for reading, except for OLD. OLD means exclusive access, so no other job or user can read it while you are using it.

2. You need a dataset just like another:

```
"ALLOC DDN(ddname) NEW REUSE DSN('dataset-to-write')" ,
    "LIKE('dataset-name-used-as-a-model')"
```

The LIKE creates a new dataset just like another one. Everything is the same except the disk volume and the data contents. If the new dataset exists already, you should use the ALLOC shown in #1 just above, instead. If you don't know if it exists you may use this REXX code:

```
DSN = "'dataset-to-write'"
IF SYSDSN(DSN) = "OK"
THEN
"ALLOC DDN(DDNAME) OLD REUSE DSN("DSN")"
ELSE
"ALLOC DDN(DDNAME) NEW REUSE DSN("DSN")" ,
        "LIKE ('dataset-name-used-as-a-model')"
```

3. There is no model dataset. My advice is to allocate the dataset using TSO ISPF option 3.2 before running the program.

Or you can do the full ALLOCATE:

```
"ALLOC DDN(ddname) NEW REUSE DSN('dataset-to-write') " ,
  "LRECL(record-length) RECFM(F B) SPACE(10 10) TRACKS"
```

It's a good idea to use the logic shown just above, with SYSDSN, like this:

```
DSN = "'dataset-name-to-write'"
IF SYSDSN(DSN) = "OK"
   THEN
     "ALLOC DDN(DDNAME) OLD REUSE DSN("DSN")"
   ELSE
     "ALLOC DDN(DDNAME) NEW REUSE DSN("DSN")" ,
       "LRECL(record-length) RECFM(F B) SPACE(10 10) TRACKS"
```

See the examples of writing to a dataset on the next left-hand page.

12.5 Writing

After a valid ALLOCATE with either NEW or OLD as a disposition, (both request exclusive access) you OPENFILE OUTPUT. This declares that you will write records to the dataset. By opening for output, you are replacing everything that is in the dataset.

The name of the output record (output record variable) is the same as the name of the file handle, (DDNAME) OUTFILE in this example. You set the output record equal to the data that you want to write.

You then PUTFILE the file handle.

When you have no more records to write, you CLOSFILE and then FREE the file handle.

Example of writing three records to a file that already exists, overwriting it.

```
/* CLST0053 TO ILLUSTRATE WRITING THREE RECORDS */
CONTROL LIST CONLIST
ALLOCATE DDN(OUTFILE) OLD REUSE DSN('userid.TEST2.DATA')
OPENFILE OUTFILE OUTPUT
SET OUTFILE = RECORD1 WILL BE WRITTEN
PUTFILE OUTFILE
SET OUTFILE = RECORD2 WILL BE WRITTEN
PUTFILE OUTFILE
SET OUTFILE = RECORD3 WILL BE WRITTEN
PUTFILE OUTFILE

CLOSFILE OUTFILE
FREE DDN(OUTFILE)
```

Example of looping, asking for input, and writing that as a record.
Stops when user presses ENTER without entering anything.

```
/* CLST0054 TO ILLUSTRATE WRITING RECORDS WITH A DO LOOP */
CONTROL LIST CONLIST
ALLOCATE DDN(OUTFILE) OLD REUSE DSN('userid.TEST2.DATA')
OPENFILE OUTFILE OUTPUT

SET STOP = NO
DO UNTIL &STOP = STOP
    WRITE IN THE LOOP
    TIME
    WRITE ENTER A LINE OF DATA TO BE WRITTEN. JUST ENTER, TO STOP
    READ DATA
    IF &DATA = THEN SET STOP = STOP
    ELSE DO /* DATA = NULL */
        SET OUTFILE = &DATA
        PUTFILE OUTFILE
    END      /* DATA = NULL */
END /* DO UNTIL */
CLOSFILE OUTFILE
FREE DDN(OUTFILE)
```

Writing in REXX

After a valid ALLOCATE with either NEW or OLD as a disposition, (both request exclusive access) you do an EXECIO DISKW. This opens the dataset for output, if it's not already open, and writes a record.

The name of the output record (output record variable) is what's specified in the STEM keyword. You may use a different name, and it doesn't need to be the same as the DDNAME.

You make the output record variable equal to the data that you want to write.

You then do an EXECIO DISKW.

When you have no more records to write, you do an EXECIO 0 DISKW with the FINIS option.

Example of writing three records to a dataset that already exists, overwriting it.

```
/* REXX0053 TO ILLUSTRATE WRITING THREE RECORDS */
TRACE C
"ALLOCATE DDN(OUTFILE) OLD REUSE DSN('userid.TEST2.DATA')"
OUTFILE.1 ="RECORD1 WILL BE WRITTEN"
"EXECIO 1 DISKW OUTFILE (STEM OUTFILE.)"
OUTFILE.1 ="RECORD2 WILL BE WRITTEN"
"EXECIO 1 DISKW OUTFILE (STEM OUTFILE.)"
OUTFILE.1 ="RECORD3 WILL BE WRITTEN"
"EXECIO 1 DISKW OUTFILE (STEM OUTFILE.)"

"EXECIO 0 DISKW OUTFILE (FINIS)"
"FREE DDN(OUTFILE)"
```

Example of looping, asking for input, and writing that as a record.

Stops when user presses ENTER without entering anything. There are other ways of doing it. I'm keeping the REXX code as close the CLIST code as possible.

```
/* REXX0054 TO ILLUSTRATE WRITING RECORDS WITH A DO LOOP */
TRACE C
"ALLOCATE DDN(OUTFILE) OLD REUSE DSN('userid.TEST2.DATA')"

STOP = "NO"
DO UNTIL STOP = "STOP"
    SAY "IN THE LOOP"
    "TIME"
    SAY "ENTER A LINE OF DATA TO BE WRITTEN. JUST ENTER, TO STOP"
    PULL DATA
    IF DATA = "" THEN STOP = "STOP"
    ELSE DO /* DATA NOT NULL */
         OUTFILE.1 = DATA
         "EXECIO 1 DISKW OUTFILE (STEM OUTFILE.)"
    END      /* DATA NOT NULL */
END /* DO UNTIL */

"EXECIO 0 DISKW OUTFILE (FINIS)"
"FREE DDN(OUTFILE)"
```

12.6 Syntax Summary for OPENFILE, GETFILE, PUTFILE, CLOSFILE and EXECIO

OPENFILE
- After a valid ALLOCATE you may open a file. The ALLOCATE specified a DDNAME. Use that on the OPENFILE.
- The format of the OPENFILE is:
  OPENFILE DDNAME INPUT
  OPENFILE DDNAME OUTPUT
  or
  OPENFILE DDNAME UPDATE
- The DDNAME may be contained in a variable.

GETFILE
- GETFILE reads a record from the dataset referenced in the ALLOCATE command and makes the entire record available in a variable whose name is equal to the DDNAME.
- GETFILE is for existing files opened as INPUT or UPDATE.
- An end of file exception is an error, and sets the variable &LASTCC to 400.
- Data is uppercased, unless a CONTROL NOCAPS or CONTROL ASIS is in effect.

PUTFILE
- PUTFILE writes a record to the dataset referenced in the ALLOCATE command, taking the data from a variable whose name is equal to the DDNAME.
- PUTFILE is for datasets opened as OUTPUT or UPDATE.
- Data is uppercased, unless a CONTROL NOCAPS or CONTROL ASIS is in effect.

CLOSFILE
- When finished with a dataset, you must close it.
- If you don't close a dataset you will not be able to FREE it; this may prevent other users, and you, from using the dataset again.

Chapter 12: File IO

EXECIO

EXECIO acts as a TSO command: it must be in quotes, except for any variables used on the command.

The general format of EXECIO is:
"EXECIO *how-many type-of-open ddname* (*options*)"

how-many	number of lines to read or write. "*" on a read means "entire file", on a write, it means "write until a null line is attempted to be written" I do not use it on a write. You can specify 0, in which case you are probably doing a FINIS (below).
type-of-open	DISKR to open for input and/or read DISKW to open for output and/or write DISKRU to open for update
ddname	the DDNAME specified on the ALLOCATE command
options	can be STEM and/or FINIS and/or FIFO-LIFO *options* are in a set of parentheses, an open, and a close parenthesis.
STEM	specifies a variable with a period (dot) that will become the stem of a set of compound variables prefixed with the variable name and suffixed with a number corresponding to the sequence number of the record being read or written If STEM is omitted, data is taken from the stack (Internal Data Queue) on a write, or is put on the stack on a read.
FINIS	closes the file after doing the operation specified on the EXECIO
FIFO-LIFO	If you aren't using STEM, this controls how data is read into the stack (Data Queue) either first-in-first-out or last-in-first-out. FIFO is the default.

- An instruction that just closes a file would look like this:
  "EXECIO 0 DISKR INFILE (FINIS) "
  It needs to specify DISKR, DISKW or DISKRU and the DDNAME.
- There is no need to omit the closing parenthesis.
- If you don't close a file you can't FREE it, possibly locking other users out of the file.

Chapter 12: File IO

This page intentionally left blank

Chapter 13: Programs Converted from CLIST to REXX, with Explanations

Chapter 13 contains working CLIST programs converted to REXX. Annotations explain the language differences.

Chapter 13 contains:

Chapter 13: Programs Converted from CLIST to REXX, with Explanations

13.1 Quick Status Program (CLIST)

This program gives you a quick summary of the jobs that you have submitted, and their place in the execution queue.

It uses SYSOUTTRAP and a DO WHILE loop.

```
/* CLST0055. QUICK STATUS.                                        */
/* EXECUTES the TSO COMMAND STATUS, CAPTUREs THE DISPLAYED OUTPUT, */
/* LOOPS THROUGH THE OUTPUT,                                       */
/* AND IF THE MESSAGE IS NO JOBS FOUND, IT EXITS                   */
/* IT LOOPS AGAIN, COUNTING THE NUMBER OF JOBS IN EACH STATUS      */
SET EXECUTING_CTR = 0
SET WAIT_CTR      = 0
SET OUTPUT_CTR    = 0
SET SYSOUTTRAP    = 100    /* ARBITRARILY CHOOSING 100 LINES. */
STATUS                     /* GET NAMES OF JOBS AND INFO ABOUT THEM */
SET SYSOUTTRAP    = 0                  /* TURN OFF CAPTURING. */
SET MAX_RETURNED = &SYSOUTLINE  /* HOW MANY LINES RETURNED */
SET INDEX = 0
DO INDEX = 1 TO &MAX_RETURNED
        SET INDEX = &INDEX + 1          /* INCREMENT INDEX */
        SET CURRENT_LINE = &STR(&&SYSOUTLINE&INDEX) /* NOTE 1 */
        /* WRITE LINE RETRIEVED IS &STR(&CURRENT_LINE) */
        IF &SYSINDEX(NO JOBS FOUND,&CURRENT_LINE,1) GT 0 THEN +
        DO
            WRITE YOU HAVE NO JOBS IN THE SYSTEM NOW
            EXIT
        END /* NO JOBS FOUND */
END /* END DO WHILE */
SET INDEX = 0
DO WHILE &INDEX LE &MAX_RETURNED
        SET INDEX = &INDEX + 1          /* INCREMENT INDEX */
        SET CURRENT_LINE = &STR(&&SYSOUTLINE&INDEX) /* NOTE 1 */
        /* WRITE LINE RETRIEVED IS &STR(&CURRENT_LINE) */
                                        /* NOTE 2 */
        IF &SYSINDEX(EXECUTING,&CURRENT_LINE,1) GT 0 THEN +
           SET EXECUTING_CTR = &EXECUTING_CTR + 1

        IF &SYSINDEX(OUTPUT QUEUE,&CURRENT_LINE,1) GT 0 THEN +
           SET OUTPUT_CTR = &OUTPUT_CTR + 1

        IF &SYSINDEX(WAITING FOR,&CURRENT_LINE,1) GT 0 THEN +
           SET WAIT_CTR = &WAIT_CTR + 1

END /* END DO WHILE */
 WRITE EXECUTING                &EXECUTING_CTR
 WRITE ON OUTPUT QUEUE          &OUTPUT_CTR
 WRITE WAITING FOR EXECUTION &WAIT_CTR
```

Note 1: This is how a nested variable is done. First &INDEX is resolved and the number is placed next to &&SYSOUTLINE. Then "&SYSOUTLINE1" (or other number) is placed in CURRENT_LINE. &CURRENT_LINE is resolved after that, and the value of the current line is retrieved.

Note 2: We use &SYSINDEX to determine if a character string is found in CURRENT_LINE. &SYSINDEX is functionally equivalent to REXX POS.

Chapter 13: Programs Converted from CLIST to REXX, with Explanations

Quick Status Program (REXX)

```
/*REXX REXX0055  - STQUICK
 COUNT AND STATUS OF JOBS SUBMITTED BY YOU
*/
CALL OUTTRAP "LINE.","*"   /* note 1 */
"STATUS"
CALL OUTTRAP "OFF"          /* note 2 */
MAX_RETURNED = LINE.0

EXECUTING_CTR = 0
WAIT_CTR      = 0
OUTPUT_CTR    = 0

DO I = 1 TO MAX_RETURNED         /* note 3 */
   IF POS("NO JOBS FOUND",LINE.I) > 0
   THEN
     DO
       SAY "YOU HAVE NO JOBS IN THE SYSTEM NOW"
       EXIT
     END
END I

DO I = 1 MAX_RETURNED            /* note 4 */
   IF POS("EXECUTING",LINE.I) > 0
      THEN EXECUTING_CTR =   EXECUTING_CTR + 1
   IF POS("OUTPUT QUEUE",LINE.I) > 0
      THEN OUTPUT_CTR =      OUTPUT_CTR    + 1
   IF POS("WAITING FOR",LINE.I) > 0
      THEN WAIT_CTR =        WAIT_CTR      + 1
END I

SAY "EXECUTING"             EXECUTING_CTR
SAY "ON OUTPUT QUEUE"       OUTPUT_CTR
SAY "WAITING FOR EXECUTION" WAIT_CTR
```

Note 1: It executes the OUTTRAP function to capture the displayed output of the TSO command STATUS. The output is not displayed on the screen. "*" means that all lines are to be captured.
Each line of the output of STATUS is placed in an element of "LINE.". The first line is placed in LINE.1, the second in LINE.2, etc. After the last line is captured, the line count is placed in LINE.0.
MAX_RETURNED is made equal to line.0.
Note 2: Turn off capturing of command output.
Note 3: The first loop checks for the words "NO JOBS FOUND". If that is in the display, the program tells you and exits.
Note 4: The second loop walks through the lines of the displayed output, and adds to a counter, determined by what is in the display.
These two loops could have been consolidated into one loop, but the program would have become more complicated. I thought it best to separate them rather than have two dissimilar logic structures in the same loop.
Future releases of TSO may display slightly different information, and this program will need to be changed. This is not very likely to happen.

Chapter 13: Programs Converted from CLIST to REXX, with Explanations

13.2 Program to Cancel Batch Jobs (CLIST)

The TSO CANCEL command has a syntax that leads to frequent errors. To avoid errors, and wasting time, this program displays the information that you need to know in order to cancel. You then type in simple information to cancel your job.

```
/* CLST0056 - CANJOB
/*
/* PURPOSE: DOES A STATUS, THEN ASKS YOU FOR JOB SUFFIX,
/*          AND JES JOB NUMBER
/*          THEN CANCELS THE JOB WITH A PURGE
/*
/* USE: %CLST0056
/*      THEN REPLY WITH JOB SUFFIX,
/*      I.E. LETTER/NUMBER APPENDED TO YOUR USERID ON JOB NAME
/*      AND JES JOB NUMBER, NUMERIC PART ONLY
/*
/*      FOR EXAMPLE:
/*
/*        %CLST0056
/*        - MESSAGE APPEARS: TSOU01A(JOB01234) EXECUTING
/*        A   1234  */

STATUS
WRITE TO CANCEL ONE OF YOUR JOBS,
 WRITE - TYPE IN:
 WRITE - JOB SUFFIX     JES JOB NUMBER
 WRITE - EXAMPLE:       P   1234
 WRITE
 READ SUFFIX NUMBER
 IF &SUFFIX = THEN +
    DO
       WRITE NEED JOB SUFFIX AND JOB NUMBER, NO COMMAS
       EXIT
    END
 IF &SUFFIX = THEN EXIT
 IF &SUFFIX = STOP  THEN EXIT

CONTROL LIST
SET &RPAREN = )       /* note 1 */
SET &LPAREN = &STR((
CANCEL &SYSUID.&SUFFIX.&LPAREN.JOB&NUMBER&RPAREN, PURGE /* NOTE 2 */
/* The command created will be like this:
/* CANCEL useridP(JOB1234), PURGE
```

Note 1: The best way to handle putting parentheses into data is to create a variable for left parenthesis, and another for right parenthesis. This is the way to do it.

Note 2: &SYSUID is prefixed to the rest of the job name. The period is not required, but I used it to make the line easier to read. Same for &SUFFIX.

However, with &LPAREN, the period is needed to distinguish it from JOB.

Chapter 13: Programs Converted from CLIST to REXX, with Explanations

Program to Cancel Batch Jobs (REXX)

```
/* REXX REXX0056 CANJOB
    PURPOSE: DOES A STATUS, THEN ASKS YOU FOR JOB SUFFIX,
             AND JES JOB NUMBER
             THEN CANCELS THE JOB WITH A PURGE
    USE: %REXX0056
         THEN REPLY WITH JOB SUFFIX,
         I.E. LETTER/NUMBER APPENDED TO YOUR USERID ON JOB NAME
         AND JES JOB NUMBER, NUMERIC PART ONLY
         FOR EXAMPLE:
          %REXX0056
          - MESSAGE APPEARS: TSOU01A(JOB01234) EXECUTING
         A    1234
*/
"STATUS"                      /* NOTE 1 */
 SAY "TO CANCEL ONE OF YOUR JOBS,"
 SAY "- TYPE IN:"
 SAY "- JOB SUFFIX     JES JOB NUMBER " /* NOTE 2 */
 SAY "- EXAMPLE:       P   1234 "
 SAY
 PULL SUFFIX NUMBER    /* NOTE 3 */
 IF SUFFIX = ""
 THEN
    DO
       SAY "NEED JOB SUFFIX AND JOB NUMBER, NO COMMAS"
       EXIT
    END
 IF SUFFIX = "" THEN EXIT
 IF SUFFIX = "STOP"  THEN EXIT

TRACE C
                                          /* NOTE 4 */
"CANCEL" USERID() || SUFFIX || "(JOB" || NUMBER"), PURGE"
/* ALTERNATIVELY, YOU COULD HAVE DONE IT THIS WAY:
"CANCEL" USERID()""SUFFIX"(JOB"NUMBER"), PURGE"
The command created will be like this:
CANCEL useridP(JOB1234), PURGE
*/
```

Note 1: The TSO command STATUS looks in the MVS/z/OS batch job execution queue for jobs that you submitted, I.E. with a job name equal to your TSO user-id plus a letter or number suffix. It displays those jobs along with their JES job number.

Note 2: JES refers to the Job Entry Subsystem, a component of MVS/z/OS that manages jobs and their printed or spooled output. This has been tested on a system with JES2.

Note 3: This PULL instruction expects you to type in two character strings: the job suffix, and the JES job number. The program then constructs a TSO CANCEL command, using your user-id, the job suffix, and the JES job number.

Note 4: I show two ways of concatenating character strings in a TSO command. The first way, the way that is actually executed, uses the concatenation operator, "||" (hex 4F). This joins consecutive character strings, stripping blanks that were between them.

The second way uses consecutive double quotes to concatenate. It works just as well as the first way, but is harder to decipher when first seen. I put this inside of a comment.

13.3 Program to Build JCL and Submit it

```
/* CLST0057 SUBMIT JCL USING THE LINE MODE EDITOR
/*     SUBMITTING JCL FOR BATCH PROCESSING.
/*     INSERTING VARIABLE VALUES INTO THE JCL.
/*     USING THE TSO LINE MODE EDITOR TO CREATE
/*     A TEMPORARY FILE, SUBMIT IT,
/*     AND EXIT WITHOUT SAVING IT
/*
SET TEMP_FILE_NAME = '&SYSUID..TEMP.SUBMIT.CNTL'
SET PROGRAM_TO_EXECUTE = MYPROG1
SET JCL_DELIMITER = &STR(/*)

/* DELETE, IF IT EXISTS. IT'S A TEMP FILE.
/* YOU SHOULD HAVE NOTHING GOOD IN A TEMP FILE. GOODBYE.  */

CONTROL NOMSG
DELETE &TEMP_FILE_NAME
CONTROL MSG
CONTROL LIST
ALLOCATE DSN(&TEMP_FILE_NAME.) NEW REUSE TRACKS +
    SPACE(3,1) LRECL(80) RECFM(F,B) BLKSIZE(8000)

EDIT &TEMP_FILE_NAME CNTL OLD NUM EMODE
10 //&SYSUID.@ JOB (0),'TEST JOB ',
20 //            TYPRUN=SCAN,
30 //            MSGLEVEL=1,CLASS=A,NOTIFY=&SYSUID
40 //STEP1     EXEC PGM=&PROGRAM_TO_EXECUTE
50 //INFILE    DD DSN=&SYSUID..INPUT.FILE,DISP=SHR
60 //OUTFILE   DD SYSOUT=A
70 //SYSIN     DD *
80 &SYSDATE &SYSTIME
90 &JCL_DELIMITER
LIST
SUBMIT
END NOSAVE
STATUS
```

Many CLISTs were written to create, modify and submit JCL using the TSO Line Mode Editor. There are many techniques and variations of the techniques used.

You need to know what the EDIT command above does.

It enters into an edit session on the named file. There is nothing in it. To prevent the editor from going into Input Mode we said EMODE – this means Edit Mode, not Input Mode. In Input Mode everything that you type in is taken as data.

NUM means that the data is line-numbered. The line numbers will be in a part of the data that doesn't affect the functioning of the JCL.

Each of the lines with a number inserts a line of data into the file. Then we LIST them – display them on the screen, SUBMIT them to the batch system. END NOSAVE exits from the editor without saving anything.

Program to Build JCL and Submit it (REXX)

```
/* REXX REXX0057 - SUBJCL3
   SUBMITTING JCL FOR BATCH PROCESSING.
   INSERTING VARIABLE VALUES INTO THE JCL.
   USING THE TSO LINE MODE EDITOR TO CREATE
   A TEMPORARY FILE, SUBMIT IT,
   AND EXIT WITHOUT SAVING IT
*/
TEMP_FILE_NAME = "'"USERID()".TEMP.SUBMIT.CNTL'"
PROGRAM_TO_EXECUTE = "MYPROG1"
JCL_DELIMITER = "/*"
/* DELETE, IF IT EXISTS. IT'S A TEMP FILE.
   YOU SHOULD HAVE NOTHING GOOD IN A TEMP FILE. GOODBYE.
*/
CALL MSG "OFF"
"DELETE" TEMP_FILE_NAME
CALL MSG "ON"

"ALLOCATE DSN("TEMP_FILE_NAME") NEW REUSE TRACKS",
   "SPACE(3,1) LRECL(80) RECFM(F,B) BLKSIZE(8000)"

QUEUE "10 //"USERID()"A JOB (0),'TEST JOB',"
QUEUE "20 //           TYPRUN=SCAN,  "
QUEUE "30 //           MSGLEVEL=1,CLASS=A,NOTIFY="USERID()
QUEUE "40 //STEP1     EXEC PGM="PROGRAM_TO_EXECUTE
QUEUE "50 //INFILE    DD DSN="USERID()".INPUT.FILE,DISP=SHR "
QUEUE "60 //OUTFILE   DD SYSOUT=A "
QUEUE "70 //SYSIN     DD * "
QUEUE "80" DATE() TIME()
QUEUE "90" JCL_DELIMITER
QUEUE "LIST"
QUEUE "SUBMIT"
QUEUE "END NOSAVE"

"EDIT" TEMP_FILE_NAME "CNTL OLD    NUM EMODE"
"STATUS"
```

The important difference is that in REXX you have to QUEUE all the EDIT subcommands. You do not QUEUE the EDIT command.

First we QUEUE the lines of the JCL that we are creating. What we put in the REXX Internal Data Queue will be seen by the Line Mode EDIT command, later. You have to do it this way, before you execute the EDIT command. The EDIT command will look for lines of input from the user. However, by placing the lines in the Queue, we are fooling EDIT into thinking that we are typing the lines in.

Notice that the EDIT command is not queued. It's executed near the end of the REXX program. When it starts, it reads what's in the queue.

Everything else in this REXX program is logically equivalent to what's in the CLIST.

13.4 Program to Calculate Square Root

This program illustrates the use of a CLIST subprocedure and a loop that increments a variable to an upper limit.

```
/* CLST0058 CALCULATE SQUARE ROOT OF A NUMBER         */
/* IN A SUBPROCEDURE                                  */
 SET RESULT = 0
 SYSCALL SQRT 64   RESULT
 WRITE THE SQUARE ROOT IS &RESULT

 EXIT /* LOGICAL END OF PROGRAM (NOT NEEDED) */

 SQRT: PROC 2 NUMBER RESULT_DATA
 SYSREF RESULT_DATA
 SET GUESS = &NUMBER / 2

 DO I = 1 TO 50
    SET NEW_GUESS = (&GUESS + (&NUMBER / &GUESS)) / 2
    SET GUESS = &NEW_GUESS
 END /* DO I = 1 TO 50 */

 SET RESULT_DATA = &NEW_GUESS
 END /* END SUBPROCEDURE */
```

The SYSCALL instruction invokes the subprocedure, passing it a number, 64, in this example. It also supplies the name of a variable, RESULT, that will contain the answer. (I could have used any other variable name instead of RESULT.)

The program loops 50 times to calculate the square root. Each iteration gets closer to the final answer. 50 iterations will produce an answer that is accurate enough for anyone.

The PROC statement picks up the variable name passed to it (RESULT). SYSREF RESULT_DATA makes RESULT_DATA in the subprocedure equal to RESULT outside of the subprocedure.

It will not calculate the square root of a negative number.

Since it does integer division, (discards remainders or non-whole numbers) the answer will not be accurate for numbers that are not squares.

Program to Calculate Square Root (REXX)

This program does everything the same way as the CLIST. The biggest difference is in the way the answer is passed back to the instruction that calls the subroutine.

This program will calculate the square root of numbers and return fractional answers, if the result is not a whole number.

```
/* REXX PROGRAM REXX0058 TO CALCULATE SQUARE ROOT */
/* ILLUSTRATE A USER-WRITTEN  FUNCTION OR SUBROUTINE */
CALL SQRT 64
SAY RESULT
EXIT /* LOGICAL END OF PROGRAM */


SQRT: /* SQRT FUNCTION OR SUBROUTINE*/
ARG NUMBER
GUESS = NUMBER / 2
IF NUMBER < 0 THEN DO
    SAY "NUMBER MUST BE POSITIVE"
RETURN 0
END



IF DATATYPE(NUMBER) = "CHAR" THEN DO
    SAY "NUMBER MUST BE NUMERIC"
RETURN 0
END

DO 50
    NEW_GUESS = (GUESS + (NUMBER / GUESS)) / 2
    GUESS = NEW_GUESS
END
RETURN NEW_GUESS /* LOGICAL END OF SUBROUTINE */
```

13.5 Editor Macro to Hide Lines

This is an ISPF Editor macro. It can be executed only in an Editor session. It will exclude (hide) all lines containing the specified character string.

```
/* CLST0059 - $HIDEALL MACRO                          */
/* A MACRO FOR THE TSO/ISPF EDITOR.                   */
/* USED WITHIN A TSO/ISPF EDIT SESSION.               */
/* I SUGGEST YOU RENAME IT $HIDEALL                   */
/* IT EXCLUDES (HIDES) ALL LINES OF THE FILE WHICH    */
/* CONTAIN A SPECIFIC CHARACTER STRING.               */
/* TO USE, WITHIN A TSO/ISPF EDIT SESSION,            */
/* TYPE $HIDEALL CHARACTER-STRING ON THE COMMAND LINE. */
/* EXAMPLE:                                           */
/* $HIDEALL DSN=                                      */


ISREDIT MACRO (PARM1)

IF &LASTCC GT 0 THEN GOTO NOT_AS_A_MACRO
IF &PARM1 = THEN EXIT
ISREDIT EXCLUDE ALL
ISREDIT FIND ALL '&PARM1'
ISREDIT FLIP
EXIT /* NORMAL END OF PROGRAM */

NOT_AS_A_MACRO: +
WRITE THIS IS A TSO/ISPF EDITOR MACRO
WRITE IT MAY BE EXECUTED ONLY IN THE ISPF EDITOR
WRITE BY TYPING $HIDEALL CHAR-STRING ON THE COMMAND LINE
EXIT
```

A macro has to declare that it is a macro with the subcommand MACRO. ISREDIT passes the subcommand to the ISPF Editor. (PARM1) picks up anything specified on the command line to the right of the macro name.

You execute it on the command line of the Editor *without* prefixing it with the word TSO.

If you are executing it outside of the Editor, or in Native Mode TSO, or prefixed with TSO, there will be an error code which &LASTCC will pick up.

ISREDIT (and a space) prefixes all subcommand that you want to pass to the editor.

If you want to talk to ISPF, you prefix the ISPF command with ISPEXEC (and a space).

If you had wanted to talk to TSO, you would simply enter the TSO command as in other CLISTs.

Chapter 13: Programs Converted from CLIST to REXX, with Explanations

Editor Macro to Hide Lines (REXX)

```
/* REXX REXX0059 - EDITOR MACRO $HIDEALL
A MACRO FOR THE TSO/ISPF EDITOR.
USED WITHIN A TSO/ISPF EDIT SESSION.
IT EXCLUDES (HIDES) ALL LINES OF THE FILE WHICH
CONTAIN A SPECIFIC CHARACTER STRING.
I SUGGEST YOU RENAME IT $HIDEALL

TO USE, WITHIN A TSO/ISPF EDIT SESSION,
TYPE $HIDEALL CHARACTER-STRING ON THE COMMAND LINE.
EXAMPLE:
$HIDEALL DSN=
*/
ADDRESS ISREDIT "MACRO (PARM1)"

IF RC > 0 THEN SIGNAL NOT_AS_A_MACRO
IF PARM1 = "" THEN EXIT
ADDRESS ISREDIT "EXCLUDE ALL"
ADDRESS ISREDIT "FIND ALL '"PARM1"'"
ADDRESS ISREDIT "FLIP "
EXIT /* NORMAL END OF PROGRAM */

NOT_AS_A_MACRO:
SAY "THIS IS A TSO/ISPF EDITOR MACRO"
SAY "IT MAY BE EXECUTED ONLY IN THE ISPF EDITOR"
SAY "BY TYPING $HIDEALL CHAR-STRING ON THE COMMAND LINE"
EXIT
```

This is a very straightforward conversion. Every feature in the CLIST has its equivalent in this REXX program. We are simply converting language elements.
Subcommands could have been sent to the ISPF Editor this way:
```
"ISREDIT  MACRO (PARM1)"

"ISREDIT EXCLUDE ALL"
"ISREDIT FIND ALL '"PARM1"'"
"ISREDIT FLIP "
```
It works equally well, and is closer to the CLIST method. I do it the way shown in the full example above.

This page intentionally left blank

Supplement 1: TSO Line Mode (Ready Mode) Command Summary

This supplement summarizes the TSO Line Mode commands that you are likely to use or find in a CLIST or a REXX program. It gives you the commands, the operands and the keywords that you need, to understand a CLIST and convert it to a REXX program. Unlike the vendor manuals, it shows you working, realistic examples of code embedded in CLISTs as well as REXX programs. It does not show you the advanced options of the commands. If you know what those options mean, you do not need this supplement, and you will know what to code.

Supplement 1 contains:

Supplement 1: TSO Line Mode (Ready Mode) Command Summary

S1.1 Specifying Dataset Names in TSO Commands

- Many TSO commands act on datasets. You will need to specify dataset names in those commands. There are a few things to remember:
- If you are specifying the full dataset name, as you would in JCL, you need to put the name in apostrophes.
  Example:
  JCL dataset name, in context:
  ```
  //INFILE    DD   DSNAME=MYUSERID.TEST1.DATA,DISP=SHR
  ```
  That dataset name on a TSO command:
  ```
  ALLOCATE DDNAME(INFILE) SHR DSNAME('MYUSERID.TEST1.DATA')
  ```
  If you omit the apostrophes, TSO will prefix the name specified, with your TSO user-id, or the character string that you specified on a TSO PROFILE PREFIX(char-string) command.
- Most CLISTs and REXX programs need to be generic: to work for all users. Consequently they will probably specify dataset names with apostrophes.
- The problem arises from the fact that apostrophes are sometimes handled one way, sometimes another way, in CLISTs and REXX programs. It's a good idea to write your CLIST or REXX program so that the user needs to specify dataset names according to the standard conventions. When in doubt, tell the user clearly what is needed: "Please enter dataset name, fully qualified, with apostrophes" or "Please enter dataset name, fully qualified, with no apostrophes."
- In a CLIST, apostrophes will be taken as part of the character string:
  Example:
  ```
  SET THE_DSN = 'MYUSERID.TEST1.DATA'
  DELETE &THE_DSN
  ```
- Apostrophes are a literal delimiter in REXX. When specifying apostrophes, you will need to specify quotes as well:
  Example:
  ```
  THE_DSN = "'MYUSERID.TEST1.DATA'"
  DELETE THE_DSN
  ```
- In a CLIST, a READ, and a READ followed by READDVAL will both lose the apostrophes, if they are typed in, but the PROC statement will keep the apostrophes, if they are typed in.
- In REXX, both the ARG and the PULL will keep the apostrophes, if they are typed in.

S1.2 ALLOCATE
Function of command.

ALLOCATE serves these main purposes:

1. To link a DDNAME (a file handle, a name by which the program opens the file) to the actual data. (An existing disk file, or the terminal, or a file that is being spooled to the printing system.)
   The link remains in effect until you do a FREE, or end your TSO session.
2. To link a DDNAME to an existing disk dataset in order for it to be extended when records are written. (MOD). The link remains in effect until you do a FREE, or end your TSO session.
3. To create a disk dataset, allocating space on the disk, and cataloguing the dataset, and, optionally, linking a DDNAME, as in 1, above. The disk dataset is permanent and catalogued.
4. To block all actual IO to or from a DDNAME, so that records written are discarded, and a READ request returns an Empty File Exception on the first READ. (DUMMY).

ALLOCATE is the online equivalent of a JCL DD statement. Essentially all the functions available in a DD statement are available in the ALLOCATE command.

It does not create VSAM datasets. You need to use the program IDCAMS for that. (Although the LIKE keyword will create a VSAM dataset like another.)

S1.2A Linking a DDNAME to an existing dataset as input to a program. (Read only.)
The dataset may be Sequential (QSAM), VSAM, PDS/PDSE or a PDS/PDSE member).

allocate ddname(*inddname*) shr reuse dsname('*the-input-dataset*')

- *inddname* is the name used in the program for opening and/or reading.
- *the-input-dataset* is the name of the actual disk dataset
- SHR means that you don't mind if other users or jobs are reading the dataset at the same time
- REUSE means that the DDNAME is released first (FREE) if it is already in use. If it is not in use, nothing happens. It may be abbreviated to REU.
- DDNAME may be abbreviated to DDN; you may use FILE or FI as well.
- DSNAME may be abbreviated to DSN; you may use DATASET or DA as well.

Example in a CLIST:
```
SET DATASET = 'userid.ABC.DATA'
ALLOCATE DDNAME(INFILE) SHR REUSE DSNAME(&DATASET
```

Example in REXX:
```
DATASET = "'userid.ABC.DATA'"
"ALLOCATE DDNAME(INFILE) SHR REUSE DSNAME("DATASET")"
```

ALLOCATE, continued
S1.2B Linking a DDNAME to an existing file as output from a program. (The file is overwritten: destroyed) Sequential datasets (QSAM) only.

allocate ddname(*outddname*) OLD reuse dsname('*the-output-dataset*')

- *outddname* is the name used in the program for opening and/or writing
- *the-output-dataset* is the name of the actual disk dataset
- OLD means that you want exclusive access: no other users or jobs can ALLOCATE the dataset.
- REUSE means that the DDNAME is released first (FREE) if it is already in use. If it is not in use, nothing happens. It may be abbreviated to REU.
- DDNAME may be abbreviated to DDN; you may use FILE or FI as well.
- DSNAME may be abbreviated to DSN; you may use DATASET or DA as well.

Example in a CLIST:
```
SET DATASET = 'userid.ABC.DATA'
ALLOCATE DDNAME(OUTFILE) OLD REUSE DSNAME(&DATASET)
```

Example in REXX:
```
DATASET = "'userid.ABC.DATA'"
"ALLOCATE DDNAME(OUTFILE) OLD REUSE DSNAME("DATASET")"
```

S1.2C Linking a DDNAME to an existing VSAM file as output from a program.
VSAM datasets. (Note: the ALLOCATE is exactly the same as for a VSAM dataset as input.)

allocate ddname(*outddname*) SHR reuse dsname('*the-output-dataset*')

- *outddname* is the name used in the program for opening and/or writing
- *the-output-dataset* is the name of the actual disk dataset
- SHR means that you don't mind if other users or jobs are reading the dataset at the same time. VSAM handles concurrent access from other users. You specify SHR.
- REUSE means that the DDNAME is released first (FREE) if it is already in use. If it is not in use, nothing happens. It may be abbreviated to REU.
- DDNAME may be abbreviated to DDN; you may use FILE or FI as well.
- DSNAME may be abbreviated to DSN; you may use DATASET or DA as well.

Example in a CLIST:
```
SET DATASET = 'userid.ABC.DATA'
ALLOCATE DDNAME(OUTFILE) SHR REUSE DSNAME(&DATASET)
```

Example in REXX:
```
DATASET = "'userid.ABC.DATA'"
 "ALLOCATE DDNAME(OUTFILE) SHR REUSE DSNAME("DATASET")"
```

<u>ALLOCATE, continued</u>
S1.2D Linking a DDNAME to an existing PDS/PDSE member as output from a program. (It is overwritten: destroyed)
PDS/PDSE member. (Note: the ALLOCATE is exactly the same as for a PDS/PDSE member as input.)

allocate ddname(*outddname*) SHR reuse dsname('*the-output-pdspdse*(*member*)')

- *outddname* is the name used in the program for opening and/or writing
- *the-output-pdspdse* is the name of the actual PDS/PDSE.
- *member* is the name of the member in the PDS/PDSE.
- SHR refers to the PDS/PDSE, not to the member. Under some conditions other users can read and/or write to the same member that you are accessing. TSO will lock other TSO users out of the member.
- REUSE means that the DDNAME is released first (FREE) if it is already in use. If it is not in use, nothing happens. It may be abbreviated to REU.
- DDNAME may be abbreviated to DDN; you may use FILE or FI as well.
- DSNAME may be abbreviated to DSN; you may use DATASET or DA as well.

Example in a CLIST:
```
SET THEINPUTPDSPDSE = &STR('userid.ABC.LIB(MEMBABC1)')
WRITE &THEINPUTPDSPDSE WILL BE ALLOCATED
ALLOCATE DDNAME(OUTFILE) SHR REUSE DSNAME(&THEINPUTPDSPDSE)
```

Example in REXX:
```
THEINPUTPDSPDSE = "'userid.ABC.LIB(MEMBABC1)'"
SAY THEINPUTPDSPDSE "WILL BE ALLOCATED"
"ALLOCATE DDNAME(OUTFILE) SHR REUSE DSNAME("THEINPUTPDSPDSE")"
```

ALLOCATE, continued
S1.2E Link a DDNAME to non-existent data: throw-away data.
WRITEs do not actually transfer data, but return a successful return code. READs receive an indication that the file is at end.

allocate ddname(*filename*) DUMMY
In some situations you will need to specify record length, blocksize and record format.

- *filename* is the name used in the program for opening, reading or writing

Example in a CLIST:
```
ALLOCATE DDNAME(OUTFILE) DUMMY
```

Example in REXX:
```
"ALLOCATE DDNAME(OUTFILE) DUMMY"
```

S1.2F Linking a DDNAME to an existing file, to extend it. (The new data is appended to the end of the existing data.) (MOD).
Sequential files (QSAM) only.

allocate ddname(*outddname*) mod reuse dsname('*the-output-dataset*')

- *outddname* is the name used in the program for opening and/or writing
- *the-output-dataset* is the name of the actual disk dataset
- MOD searches for the dataset. If found, data is appended. If not found, the dataset is created (so you would need SPACE and other parameters used for creating.) MOD implies exclusive access: no other users or jobs can ALLOCATE the dataset.
- REUSE means that the DDNAME is released first (FREE) if it is already in use. If it is not in use, nothing happens. It may be abbreviated to REU.
- DDNAME may be abbreviated to DDN; you may use FILE or FI as well.
- DSNAME may be abbreviated to DSN; you may use DATASET or DA as well.

Example in a CLIST:
```
SET DATASET = 'userid.ABC.DATA'
ALLOCATE DDNAME(OUTFILE) MOD REUSE DSNAME(&DATASET)
```

Example in REXX:
```
DATASET = "'userid.ABC.DATA'"
"ALLOCATE DDNAME(OUTFILE) MOD REUSE DSNAME("DATASET")"
```

ALLOCATE, continued
S1.2G Linking a DDNAME to the terminal, as input or output.
If you are using the terminal for input, be advised that:
There is no indication that the program is trying to read a record and is waiting for you to type it in.
/* is the end of file delimiter.
You have no control over record length, blocksize or record format.

allocate ddname(*filename*) reuse dsn(*)

- *filename* is the name used in the program for opening, reading or writing

Example in a CLIST:
```
ALLOCATE DDNAME(INFILE) REUSE DSN(*)
```

Example in REXX:
```
"ALLOCATE DDNAME(INFILE) REUSE DSN(*)"
```

S1.2H Linking a DDNAME to the printer spooling system
With this, you can send a file to the printer system, directly from your terminal.

allocate ddname(*outddname*) reuse sysout(*sysoutclass*) dest(*destination*)

- *outddname* is the name used in the program for opening and/or writing
- *sysoutclass* defined by your installation. You have to find out what is appropriate for you to use.
- *destination* defined by your installation. You have to find out what is appropriate for you to use.

Example in a CLIST:
```
ALLOCATE DDNAME(INFILE) SYSOUT(A) DEST(DEPT1)
```

Example in REXX:
```
"ALLOCATE DDNAME(INFILE) SYSOUT(A) DEST(DEPT1) "
```

ALLOCATE, continued
S1.2I Creating a sequential file (QSAM) and optionally linking a DDNAME to an existing file as output.
Sequential (QSAM).

allocate ddname(*outddname*) new reuse dsname('*the-new-dataset*') space(*primary secondary*)
space-type

- *outddname* is the name used in the program for opening and/or writing
  Omit DDNAME(*outddname)* if you are not going to write to the dataset now.
- *the-new-dataset* is the name of the dataset that you are creating. If you want a temporary dataset
  omit the DSNAME parameter. Then add the keyword DELETE.
- NEW means that it doesn't exist. However, if it does, it is an error and your program will fail.
- REUSE means that the DDNAME is released first (FREE) if it is already in use. If it is not in use, nothing
  happens. It may be abbreviated to REU.
- DDNAME may be abbreviated to DDN; you may use FILE or FI as well.
- DSNAME may be abbreviated to DSN; you may use DATASET or DA as well.
- SPACE requests disk space, and implies NEW.
- *primary* how much space to allocate initially
- *secondary* how much space to allocate repeatedly when the primary is filled
- *space-type* is TRACKS, CYLINDERS or BLOCK (number of blocks for which you need space).
  BLOCK is NOT blocksize.

Example in a CLIST:
```
ALLOCATE DDNAME(OUTFILE) NEW REUSE DSNAME('userid.MY.NEW.DATA') +
SPACE(10 10) TRACKS
```

Example in REXX:
```
"ALLOCATE DDNAME(OUTFILE) NEW REUSE DSNAME('userid.MY.NEW.DATA')"
```

ALLOCATE, continued
S1.2J Creating a PDS/PDSE. This is NOT for creating a member. Use S1.4 above for that.
Consider doing this using ISPF 3.3 instead.

allocate dsname('*name-of-pdspdse*') new space(*primary secondary*) +
dir(*amount*) dsorg(PO) lrecl(*record-length*) blksize(*block-size*) recfm(*record-format*)

- *name-of-pdspdse* Name of PDS/PDSE that you are creating
- NEW You are creating this. It does not already exist. Severe error if that is not true.
- SPACE request disk space, and implies NEW
- *primary* how much space to allocate initially
- *secondary* how much space to allocate repeatedly when the primary is filled
- *space-type* is TRACKS, CYLINDERS or BLOCK (number of blocks for which you need space).
- DIR This parameter says that this is a PDS/PDSE and how much space you are specifying for its directory.
- *amount* How much space you want for the directory. This implies DSORG(PO)
- DSORG(PO) This makes it explicit that you are creating a PDS/PDSE.
- *record-length* Record length of individual records.
- *block-size* Size of block that contains individual records.
- *record-format* Generally F for Fixed, or V for variable.

Example in a CLIST:
```
ALLOCATE DSNAME('userid.TESTPDS') NEW SPACE(12  2) +
DIR(2) DSORG(PO) LRECL(80) BLKSIZE(800) +
RECFM(F B)
```

Example in REXX:
```
"ALLOCATE DSNAME('userid.TESTPDS') NEW SPACE(12  2) " ,
"DIR(2) DSORG(PO) LRECL(80) BLKSIZE(800) " ,
"RECFM(F B)   "
```

ALLOCATE, continued
S1.2K Concatenating input files.
Reading two or more datasets as input, stacked one after the other, as if they all were one dataset.
This is for QSAM datasets or PDS/PDSEs. (But not both together.)

allocate ddname(*inddname*) shr reuse dsname('*dsn1*' '*dsn2*' '*dsn3*')

- *inddname* is the name used in the program for opening and/or reading.
- *the-input-dataset* is the name of the actual disk dataset
- SHR means that you don't mind if other users or jobs are reading the dataset at the same time
- REUSE means that the DDNAME is released first (FREE) if it is already in use. If it is not in use, nothing happens. It may be abbreviated to REU.
- DDNAME may be abbreviated to DDN; you may use FILE or FI as well.
- DSNAME may be abbreviated to DSN; you may use DATASET or DA as well.
- *dsn1 dsn2 dsn3* Are two or more dataset names that you are reading in as input. If one has a larger blocksize than another, put that one first. There are some situations in which that doesn't matter. This way works all the time.
  All must have the same record length and record format.

Example in a CLIST:
```
ALLOCATE DDNAME(INFILE) SHR REUSE DSNAME('userid.ABC.DATA' +
'userid.ABD.DATA' 'userid.ABE.DATA')
```

Example in REXX:
```
"ALLOCATE DDNAME(INFILE) SHR REUSE DSNAME('userid.ABC.DATA'" ,
"'userid.ABD.DATA' 'userid.ABE.DATA') "
```

S1.2L Creating a file like another.
This will work for sequential (QSAM), VSAM and PDS/PDSE.
All the attributes of the model dataset are copied to the new one, except the new name and the volume serial on which the new dataset is placed. (It may be the same or different.)
You may add other parameters if you don't want the parameters of the model dataset, for example, you may add SPACE for a different space allocation.

allocate dsname('*dataset-to-be-created*') like('*dataset-used-as-a-model*')
dataset-to-be-created The name of the new dataset.
dataset-used-as-a-model The name of an existing dataset whose attributes you are copying.

Example in a CLIST:
```
ALLOCATE DSNAME('userid.ABC.DATA') LIKE('userid.ABD.DATA')
```

Example in REXX:
```
"ALLOCATE DSNAME('userid.ABC.DATA') LIKE('userid.ABD.DATA') "
```

Supplement 1: TSO Line Mode (Ready Mode) Command Summary

S1.3 ALTLIB

- ALTLIB defines PDS/PDSEs that are searched before the default libraries.
- Its effect lasts for the duration of your TSO session.
- If you issue an ALTLIB command outside of ISPF, you will have to issue another one when you get into ISPF.
- If you issue an ALTLIB command in one half of an ISPF split screen, you will have to issue another on the other half.
- It allows you to use PDS/PDSEs for CLISTs and REXX programs without doing an ALLOCATE, or without having PDS/PDSEs defined in your logon procedure.
- Normally, TSO searches for CLISTs in PDS/PDSEs allocated to the DDNAME SYSPROC. ALTLIB makes TSO search first in the PDS/PDSEs that it specifies.
- Normally, TSO searches for REXX programs in PDS/PDSEs allocated to the DDNAME SYSEXEC. ALTLIB makes TSO search first in the PDS/PDSEs that it specifies.

The general format is:
altlib activate appl(*type*) dataset('PDS/PDSE1' 'PDS/PDSE2' 'PDS/PDSE3' etc.)
type can be
CLIST
or
EXEC, for REXX

- The blocksizes of the PDS/PDSEs are unimportant. they can be different without any problem.
- If you do the command again, after it has been done successfully, you are actually stacking definitions. This doesn't cause a problem. You can stack up to eight requests.
- You can do a deactivate first, to eliminate stacking. Doing a deactivate without needing to, is no problem.
- The example code shows deactivate then activate.

Example in a CLIST:
```
ALTLIB DEACTIVATE APPL(CLIST)
ALTLIB ACTIVATE APPL(CLIST) DATASET('PDS/PDSE1' 'PDS/PDSE2' 'PDS/PDSE3')
```

Example in REXX:
```
"ALTLIB DEACTIVATE APPL(EXEC) "
"ALTLIB ACTIVATE APPL(EXEC) DATASET('PDS/PDSE1' 'PDS/PDSE2' 'PDS/PDSE3')"
```

Another way to use ALTLIB is to allocate your PDS/PDSEs to the DDNAME SYSUPROC for CLISTs, or SYSUEXEC for REXX programs. Then you use ALTLIB to activate those DDNAMES

Example in a CLIST:
```
ALLOCATE DDNAME(SYSUPROC) SHR REUSE DSN('PDS/PDSE1' 'PDS/PDSE2' 'PDS/PDSE3')
ALTLIB ACTIVATE USER(CLIST)
```

Example in REXX:
```
"ALLOCATE DDNAME(SYSUEXEC) SHR REUSE DSN('PDS/PDSE1' 'PDS/PDSE2' 'PDS/PDSE3') "
"ALTLIB ACTIVATE USER(EXEC) "
```

Supplement 1: TSO Line Mode (Ready Mode) Command Summary

S1.4 CALL
- This is the TSO command that executes a compiled program on a PDS/PDSE. You need to specify a member name. If you don't, TSO assumes the member name TEMPNAME.
- You may pass parameters to the program. This is equivalent to the JCL PARM= parameter.
- In a CLIST, The parameters are uppercased unless you have executed a CONTROL ASIS or NOCAPS.
- In REXX, the parameters are not uppercased.
- You specify the PDS/PDSE and the member name. You may use "*" instead of the PDS/PDSE to make TSO search through all the libraries in the standard search order.
- The program can pass a number, including abend codes, back to TSO. In a CLIST, you will see it in &LASTCC and &MAXCC. In REXX, you will see it in the reserved variable RC.

S1.5 CANCEL
- You can use this to cancel batch jobs whose name is equal to your TSO user-id plus one or more characters.
- You normally do a STATUS first, to find out the job names and JES job numbers.
- You need both pieces of information.
- The general format is:
  CANCEL *userid+suffix*(JOB*jesjob#*)
- *user-id* is your TSO logon ID.
- *Suffix* is one or more characters that you appended to your TSO logon ID. (Without + sign.)
- JOB is literally "JOB"
- *jesjob#* is a number assigned to your job by the job scheduling system when you submitted it. It is a number.
- You may add the keyword PURGE to delete all printed output of the job that has not already printed. No comma is needed before PURGE.

Example in a CLIST:
```
CANCEL user-idA(JOB1234)
CANCEL user-idA(JOB1234) PURGE
```

Example in REXX:
```
"CANCEL user-idA(JOB1234)"
"CANCEL user-idA(JOB1234) PURGE"
```

S1.6 DELETE

This will delete a dataset, including a PDS/PDSE, that resides on disk. It will also uncatalog it, if it found it through the catalog. (That is how things are normally done.) Uncataloguing without deleting should be left to personnel responsible for system maintenance.

DELETE dataset or PDS/PDSE
DELETE (list of datasets or PDS/PDSEs)

You may substitute an "*" for a level:
DELETE mydata.*
Do not use "*" for the high level qualifier.

If you put DELETE in a CLIST or REXX program, be prepared for a few situations.
- Dataset does not exist. Error message. Not kicked out of CLIST. Not kicked out of REXX program.
- Dataset is open. Should have closed it.
- Other user has exclusive access.

Example in a CLIST:
```
DELETE 'dataset' or 'PDS/PDSE1'
DELETE ('PDS/PDSE1' 'dataset')
```

Example in REXX:
```
"DELETE 'dataset' 'PDS/PDSE1'"
"DELETE ('PDS/PDSE1' 'dataset') "
```

- You can delete one member of a PDS/PDSE. This will delete only the member, not the PDS/PDSE.
  ```
  DELETE 'MYUSERID.ABC.PDS(MEMBER1)'
  ```

Example in a CLIST:
```
DELETE 'MYUSERID.ABC.PDS(MEMBER1)'
```

Example in REXX:
```
"DELETE 'MYUSERID.ABC.PDS(MEMBER1)'"
```

S1.6 Line Mode EDIT

This program is used in many CLISTs and REXX programs to submit JCL for batch processing. It can create a temporary file, insert lines, make changes, submit it, and exit with or without saving the file.
Using EDIT means you don't have to allocate a dataset and write records to it with CLIST or REXX file IO.

The general format of the EDIT command:
EDIT '*dsn*' *NEW/OLD NUM/NONUM EMODE/IMODE CAPS/ASIS*

dsn	is the name of a sequential (QSAM) dataset, or a PDS/PDSE member.
NEW/OLD	NEW if the dataset doesn't exist. OLD if it exists and you want to reuse it
NUM/NONUM	NUM if it has or you want line numbers. NONUM if you don't.
EMODE/IMODE	EMODE means Edit mode, not Input mode. IMODE is Input Mode, where everything that you type in becomes a new line in the dataset. Hitting ENTER toggles between IMODE and EMODE.
CAPS/ASIS	CAPS (the default) will be needed for JCL.

Subcommands of EDIT:

TOP	set first line as current line
BOTTOM	set last line as current line
CHANGE	change data strings
END SAVE	end the EDIT session and save the dataset as specified
END NOSAVE	end the EDIT session and don't save the dataset
SAVE newname	save the dataset with a new name, not the one specified on the EDIT command
FIND	position the current line at the line containing specified data
RENUM	recalculate line numbers
SUBMIT	send the contents of the EDIT session to the batch system for processing.

For an example of EDIT in a CLIST, see program CLST0057 in Chapter 13.
For an example of EDIT in a REXX program, see program REXX0057 in Chapter 13.

Example of CHANGE
```
CHANGE 10 1000 'DNS=' 'DSN=' ALL
```

S1.8 LISTALC

- This will display the names of the datasets and PDS/PDSEs currently in use in your session. They were linked to by an ALLOCATE command, a JCL DD statement in the logon procedure, or through dynamic allocation in a program.
- You can abbreviate it LISTA
- The command without additional keywords will display the datasets and PDS/PDSEs.

You may specify additional keywords for additional information:

STATUS   Abbreviated S   DDNAMEs, dataset names, PDS/PDSE names, and the final disposition to be carried out when the ALLOCATion ends.

HISTORY   Abbreviated H   Date created, expiration date.
DSORG: whether QSAM or PDS/PDSE or other

MEMBERS   Abbreviated M   names of members in PDS/PDSEs.

Example in a CLIST:
LISTALC STATUS HISTORY MEMBERS

Example in REXX:
"LISTALC STATUS HISTORY MEMBERS"

S1.9 LISTCAT

This will display names of datasets, PDS/PDSEs, VSAM datasets and other file types that are catalogued and whose names have your user-id as a high level qualifier. You can substitute another character string for your user-id.

You can abbreviate it LISTC

The command without additional parameters will display names of files with your user-id as a high level qualifier.

You may specify additional parameters and keywords for additional information

LEVEL(a high-level qualifier, such as a user-id)
ENTRIES('a specific dataset name')
ALL   VOLUME, ALLOCATION, HISTORY
VOLUME   Volume serial numbers
ALLOCATION   for VSAM datasets
HISTORY   Creation and expiration dates
OUTFILE(datasetname)   Write output to a dataset instead of the terminal.

Example in a CLIST:
LISTCAT LEVEL(ABC1)

Example in REXX:
"LISTCAT LEVEL(ABC1)"

Supplement 1: TSO Line Mode (Ready Mode) Command Summary

S1.10 LISTDS
This will display information about a catalogued dataset.
It will display record length, block size, record format and dataset organization, DDNAMES currently linked to datasets, their creation and expiration dates, and member names in a PDS/PDSE.
Abbreviation: LISTD

Basic format:
LISTDS datasetname *options*
The options are:

STATUS	DDNAMES and disposition
HISTORY	creation and expiration date
MEMBERS	member names in a PDS/PDSE

Options can be abbreviated to the first letter.

S1.11 PROFILE
The effect of this command carries over from one session (logon) to another.
The useful options are:

PROFILE	displays the current settings
PROFILE PROMPT	allow TSO commands to prompt for missing information (default)
PROFILE NOPROMPT	do not prompt
PROFILE PREFIX(new-prefix)	use this new-prefix as the new high level qualifier for datasets specified without apostrophes.

S1.12 STATUS
Displays the current position of a submitted job in the execution queue.
The job may be EXECUTING, ON OUTPUT QUEUE or WAITING FOR EXECUTION.
It will also give the JES job number assigned when the JOB is submitted.

STATUS	with no parameters will display information for jobs whose names are your TSO user-id + one or more characters.
STATUS jobname	displays information for jobs with that specific name. There may be more than one, each with a different JES job number.
STATUS jobname(JOB9999)	displays information for that specific job.

Example in a CLIST:
STATUS

Example in REXX:
"STATUS"

S1.13 SUBMIT

This is the TSO command SUBMIT. There is also a Line Mode Editor subcommand SUBMIT.
The TSO command submits a dataset or PDS/PDSE member, or JCL immediately following it, in a CLIST.
The Line Mode Editor subcommand submits the contents of the file that is currently being edited.

Submitting a dataset or PDS/PDSE member:
SUBMIT MYLIB.CNTL(JOB0001)

Example in a CLIST:
```
SUBMIT MYLIB.CNTL(JOB0001)
```

Example in REXX:
```
"SUBMIT MYLIB.CNTL(JOB0001)"
```

Submitting JCL that immediately follows the command:
Example in a CLIST:
```
SET JCL_DELIMITER = "/*"
SUBMIT * END($$) /* You may use 2 other characters, instead of $$.*/
//userid@ JOB (0),'TEST JOB',
//          TYPRUN=SCAN,
//          MSGLEVEL=1,CLASS=A,NOTIFY=userid
//STEP1     EXEC PGM=PROGRAMA
/INFILE    DD DSN=userid.INPUT.FILE,DISP=SHR
//OUTFILE   DD SYSOUT=A
//SYSIN     DD *
&SYSDATE &SYSTIME
&JCL_DELIMITER
$$
```

Example in REXX:
```
JCL_DELIMITER = "/*"
QUEUE "//userid@ JOB (0),'TEST JOB',"
QUEUE "//          TYPRUN=SCAN, "
QUEUE "//          MSGLEVEL=1,CLASS=A,NOTIFY=userid"
QUEUE "//STEP1     EXEC PGM=PROGRAMA "
QUEUE "/INFILE     DD DSN=userid.INPUT.FILE,DISP=SHR "
QUEUE "//OUTFILE   DD SYSOUT=A "
QUEUE DATE(U) TIME()
QUEUE JCL_DELIMITER
QUEUE "$$"

"SUBMIT * END($$)" /* You may use 2 other characters, instead of $$.*/
```

S1.14 REPRO

- REPRO works for QSAM, VSAM and PDS/PDSE members. It is not the way to copy an entire PDS/PDSE to another. (I use ISPF option 3.3 for that.)
- If you need a way to copy one dataset to another, REPRO makes it easy. I suggest allocating the output dataset first, with ALLOCATE. ALLOCATE with LIKE is the best way to create an empty dataset with the same attributes as another.
- REPRO will write over the output dataset, completely replacing it.
- If the output dataset exists, the REPRO command is very easy to use.
- Example:

```
REPRO INDATASET('input dataset name') OUTDATASET('output dataset name')
```

Example in a CLIST:
```
REPRO INDATASET('input dataset name') OUTDATASET('output dataset name')
```

Example in REXX:
```
"REPRO INDATASET('input dataset name') OUTDATASET('output dataset name')"
```

- REPRO is actually executing the IDCAMS program's REPRO function.
- If there is data in the output dataset and you want to write over it, add the REUSE keyword at the end of the command.
- Example:

```
REPRO INDATASET('dsn1') OUTDATASET('dsn2') REUSE
```

Supplement 2: Definitions of Terms Used in this Book

Some words used in this book are jargon: they have no meaning, or a different meaning, outside of the world of IBM z/OS, TSO and ISPF. This chapter will be useful for someone who is familiar with programming, but not with the IBM mainframe world.

Supplement 2: Definitions of Terms Used in this Book

- **Attention Interrupt** A request by the user, to stop permanently or temporarily the processing of the program currently executing. Generally done by pressing the PA1 or the ATTN key on a standard IBM mainframe keyboard. Keyboard emulators map these keys to other, PC, keys. You have to find out what keys are used in your installation.
- **Background** A job or program that executes with no interaction with a person at a terminal. Same as Batch.
- **Batch** Same as Background.
- **Block Size** in QSAM files, there is the concept of block size. Individual records are stored next to other records. The agglomeration of records is called a block. The block size is the length in bytes of the block. For fixed format records, the block size is an integer multiple of the record length.
- **Built-in Function** A facility of the REXX language that is available for use from within your REXX program when you need it. It performs arithmetic or character string manipulation, or returns system information. It is invoked generally by a function invocation in the form
  `X = FUNCTIONNAME(parameters)`, but may also be invoked by a CALL, in which case the returned data is available in the reserved variable RESULT. Compare Function.
- **Catalog** A facility of the operating system whereby the names and locations of files, datasets, PDS/PDSE's, VSAM files and other catalogs are kept and organized for easy retrieval.
- **Command** I use *command* to mean a TSO or ISPF command or subcommand. I use *instruction* for CLIST and REXX "verbs".
- **Dataset** A collection of data, on disk or tape. In the TSO environment, a very small number of TSO users are allowed to use tapes. Can also be a virtual dataset that never actually resides on disk or tape. This is often the case for temporary datasets used in JCL.
- **Data Queue** See Stack
- **DDNAME** (same as File Handle) It is a name used in two places: 1. the program doing file IO (which can be a CLIST, a REXX program, or a program in another language such as COBOL, Assembler or C. 2. the ALLOCATE command or JCL DD statement. It links the program's file handling statements to an actual dataset, the terminal, or the printer spooling system.
- **DSNAME** The name of a dataset. (See dataset.)
- **Editor Profile** When you use the ISPF Editor, you have the ability to modify the default profile that the Editor has created for all datasets and PDS/PDSEs with the same low-level qualifier. Type PROFILE on the command line of the Editor to see and/or modify it.
- **Explicit execution** Executing your CLIST or REXX program with the EXEC command and the name of the PDS/PDSE plus name of member containing your program. Example:
  `EXEC 'PDS/PDSE(MEMBER)'`
- **File Handle** (same as DDNAME)
- **File** A generic term. It can mean a dataset (definition above) or a DDNAME. It can be a generic name that includes datasets, the terminal opened as input or output or the printer spooling system. Those are three *different* things. I will use "file" generically in this book. It can also be used to mean DDNAME I will not use it to mean DDNAME. (File handle is used for that.)
- **Foreground** An interactive session on a terminal

- **Function** In REXX, a set of code contained either inside (internal user-written) the program, or outside (external user-written). Data is passed to it through its ARG statement, and data is returned (obligatorily) on its RETURN statement. See also Built-in Function.
  It's not required to hide variables from the main part of the program. The PROCEDURE statement, which hides variables, is optional in a function. But if the function is written correctly, adding it will not change the way it works. See *also* Built-in Function.
- **Hex** The term generally used for the internal representation of data according to the EBCDIC coding scheme. A space is represented on the IBM mainframe as a hex 40, while on the PC it is hex 20.
- **Implicit execution** Executing your CLIST or REXX program by specifying only the member name, and not the PDS/PDSE in which is it located, on the command line. TSO finds the member by searching the PDS/PDSEs that you have specified to it in an ALLOCATE command. Example:
  MYREXX or %**MYREXX**
- **Instruction** I use *instruction* for a CLIST or REXX "verb" or assignment statement, such as SET or SIGNAL. *Statement* is used as well.
- **Internal Data Queue** See Stack
- **ISPF Editor** A full-screen editor optimized for program development. It is eminently suitable for the type of code commonly found on the mainframe.
- **ISPF** Interactive System Productivity Facility. A program development system that is found on TSO. It is menu driven: input fields eliminate the need for command keywords.
- **JCL Procedure** Stored and catalogued JCL code.
- **JCL** Job Control Language. The batch job definition language used on the mainframe.
- **Library** A common name for a PDS/PDSE.
- **Line Mode Editor** Before ISPF, the only editor available on TSO was this. You did not see the edited data on the screen, unless you did a LIST. You were able to change data not by typing over it, but by doing a CHANGE subcommand. It is still used in CLISTs and REXX programs to prepare and modify JCL before submission.
- **Logon procedure** A set of JCL that is executed when you log on to TSO. It defines datasets, PDS/PDSEs, and printer spooling parameters that you will use during your TSO session.
- **Loop** A program control structure that executes code repeatedly.
- **Macro** An executable file, written in CLIST or REXX, containing ISPF Editor subcommands and/or instructions that work only in macros.
- **Member** An individual file contained in a PDS/PDSE.
- **Null** A variable or a literal containing zero characters.
- **OPEN** Establishing a connection to a file, the terminal, or the spooling system, and setting up a set of information (control blocks) that is used during reading or writing.
- **Panel** (synonym for screen) A way of formatting a screen on a terminal. There are display fields and input fields. The TAB key will skip from one input field to another.
- **PDS/PDSE** A disk dataset containing smaller datasets. Each of the smaller datasets is called a member. Each member has the same record length, block size, and record format as the others.

- **QSAM** The simplest type of data set organization on the mainframe. The default kind of file that you obtain with a JCL DD statement, or a TSO ALLOCATE. It is almost always blocked (individual records stored next to other records in a block.)
- **Reading** Copying a record from a file and making it available to a program for processing.
- **Record Format** Whether each record is of the same length (fixed format) or if they may be of different lengths (variable format).
- **Record Length** How long a record is, in bytes.
- **Screen** (synonym for panel)
- **Stack** (same as Internal Data Queue). The moment the first REXX program begins to execute, memory is allocated for use with the stack. It is a temporary area of storage that REXX (and Assembler language) programs can access. Any REXX program that your REXX program calls can access the stack. When the last REXX program stops executing, all that is in the stack comes back out, and it taken by TSO as standard input, as if it had been typed in on the command line, and is executed. Data is placed in it in lines which are logically equivalent to records, since the lines may contain one or more variables or character strings. There is no practical limit to the line length. The number of lines that may be placed into it is limited by the amount of machine storage available to your program. Lines are taken from the queue by the PULL instruction (and others as well). Lines are put into it by the QUEUE instruction (FIFO) or the PUSH instruction (LIFO) (and others as well).
- **SUBMIT** Send a set of JCL to the batch system for processing.
- **Subroutine** In REXX, a set of code contained inside the program which you can execute by the REXX CALL instruction. Variables are shared by default with the rest of the program. No ARG is needed, and no data needs to be returned on the RETURN instruction. There are no external subroutines.
- **TSO** Time Sharing Option. It is an integral part of IBM's flagship operating system (not really an option). It allows access to datasets and programs that are executed at a terminal. It is the original "cloud" computing. Your terminal is just a terminal. Access is usually through a personal computer, thus combining the best qualities of the mainframe and the personal computer. Programs and data are accessed through TSO commands, although the vast majority of TSO users today use ISPF rather than execute TSO commands.
- **TSO dataset naming conventions**. When you specify a dataset or PDS/PDSE name on a TSO command you can specify it in its entirety, with apostrophes and all levels of qualification. Or you can omit the apostrophes, in which case TSO will prefix your TSO user-id (or other string that you specified in a TSO PROFILE command.) There is much confusion because of numerous CLISTs which prompt you for dataset or PDS/PDSE names without following naming conventions, sometimes asking you to type it in with apostrophes, sometimes without.
- **TSO Native Mode** Before there was ISPF, there was only Native Mode TSO. Everything was done with TSO commands and the Line Mode Editor. You execute TSO commands in a CLIST or a REXX program. Same as TSO Ready Mode, or Native Mode.
- **VSAM** A more sophisticated method of organizing datasets. Datasets are (most of the time) defined using the program IDCAMS, or with parameters of the ALLOCATE command. All VSAM datasets are catalogued. This level of reliability was required in files, before databases utilizing them could become a reality. (DB2, IMS.)
- **Writing** Creating a record on a file from information in a program.

Supplement 3: REXX Program that Mimics CLIST PROC

The CLIST initial PROC and the REXX initial ARG work differently. If you want your REXX program to do what a CLIST does when it's executed, you'll need some code. This REXX program duplicates most of the functionality of the CLIST PROC. Use it as a model if you need it.
The CLIST is on the left-hand page, and the REXX program is on several right-hand pages.

Supplement 3 contains:
    CLIST
    REXX Program

Short CLIST written to illustrate the CLIST PROC statement. Its functionality is duplicated in the REXX program starting on the facing page.

```
/* CLST0060 MODEL CLIST
/* FOR TESTING CLIST TO REXX PROC CONVERTER PROGRAM
PROC 3 NAME ADDR PHONE   STATE(NY) WEEKDAY(MONDAY) CALENDAR(GREGORIAN)
WRITE &STR(POSITIONAL PARAMETERS AS RESOLVED)
WRITE &STR(NAME) &NAME
WRITE &STR(ADDR) &ADDR
WRITE &STR(PHONE) &PHONE
WRITE &STR(KEYWORD   PARAMETERS AS RESOLVED)
WRITE &STR(STATE) &STATE
WRITE &STR(WEEKDAY) &WEEKDAY
WRITE &STR(CALENDAR) &CALENDAR
```

Discussion.
The CLIST is very short, and the REXX program is long. This is because the CLIST PROC works very differently from REXX. Additional code is needed to make REXX work something like CLIST.

REXX doesn't have a PROC, but it has ARG. It's the nearest thing but it's not the same at all. Here are some of the differences.

Look at this typical PROC:
```
PROC 3 NAME ADDR PHONE   STATE(NY) WEEKDAY(MONDAY) CALENDAR(GREGORIAN)
```

Action of the PROC statement.
It indicates how TSO should process the information typed in at the command line, when the CLIST is executed. Assume that the above PROC is in a CLIST named CLST0060, and that it is executed like this on the command line of TSO/ISPF Option 6:
==> **clst0060 john 148a 2125554583 state(pa)**

Upon execution, all of the CLIST variables will be set.
     NAME will equal "JOHN"
     ADDR will equal "148A"
     PHONE will equal "2125554583"
     STATE will equal "PA"
     WEEKDAY will equal "MONDAY"
     CALENDAR will equal "GREGORIAN"

Continued on the next left-hand page.

Supplement 3: REXX Program that Mimics CLIST PROC

This is the REXX program that duplicates most of the functionality of the CLIST on the facing page.

```
/* REXX REXX0060 TO DUPLICATE FUNCTIONALITY OF CLIST PROC

To test:

rexx0060 joe 22-elm-st 4343434
rexx0060 joe 22-elm-st 4343434 state(ct)
rexx0060 joe 22-elm-st 4343434 calendar(julian)

*/

DEBUG = "NO "                          /* YES OR NO */
SHOW_RESOLVED_VARIABLES = "YES"   /* SHOW ALL VARIABLES/PARMS SET */
ARG CMD_LINE_ENTERED       /* PICK UP WHAT'S ON COMMAND LINE */
NUM_POS_PARMS = 3          /* COUNT THE FOLLOWING    */
POS_PARM.1     = "NAME"    /* CHANGE FOR YOUR NEEDS */
POS_PARM.2     = "ADDR"    /* CHANGE FOR YOUR NEEDS */
POS_PARM.3     = "PHONE"   /* CHANGE FOR YOUR NEEDS */
POS_PARM.0     = NUM_POS_PARMS

NUM_KEY_PARMS = 3                      /* COUNT THE FOLLOWING    */
KEY_PARM.1     = "STATE(NY)"           /* CHANGE FOR YOUR NEEDS */
KEY_PARM.2     = "WEEKDAY(MONDAY)"     /* CHANGE FOR YOUR NEEDS */
KEY_PARM.3     = "CALENDAR(GREGORIAN)" /* CHANGE FOR YOUR NEEDS */
KEY_PARM.0     = 3                     /* NUMBER OF KEYW PARMS   */

CALL UNSTRING_CMD_LINE_ENTERED
CALL PARM_WAS_ENTERED_OR_ASK
CALL VERIFY_INPUT
IF SHOW_RESOLVED_VARIABLES = "YES" THEN CALL DISPLAY_INPUT
CALL PROCESS_KEYWORDS
IF SHOW_RESOLVED_VARIABLES = "YES" THEN CALL DISPLAY_INPUT_KEYWORDS
EXIT /* LOGICAL END OF PROGRAM */

UNSTRING_CMD_LINE_ENTERED: /* PICS UP BOTH POSIT AND KEYWORD PARMS */
DO I = 1 TO WORDS(CMD_LINE_ENTERED)
   POS_ENTERED.I = WORD(CMD_LINE_ENTERED, I)
END I
IF DEBUG = "YES" THEN DO I = 1 TO WORDS(CMD_LINE_ENTERED)
   SAY POS_ENTERED.I I
END
RETURN
```

REXX program continued on next right-hand page.

Supplement 3: REXX Program that Mimics CLIST PROC

Continued from previous left-hand page

All data is uppercased. All the variables named on the PROC are set to something.
"3" means that there are 3 required variables. You must enter a value for them when you execute the CLIST. If you don't, TSO will ask (prompt) you for them. Just hitting ENTER won't work. You are entering words, and there cannot be spaces in a word. Putting values in quotes doesn't work.
You must enter a non-space character. Some characters are not accepted, such as "["
You must enter them in the right order – that's why they are called "positional parameters."
The parameters after the first 3, in this example, are "keyword parameters", and they have a default value, so they don't have to be entered. If you enter one or more of them, that value will override the default value. If you don't enter one or more of them, the default values will be used. They must come after the positionals, both on the PROC and on the command line during execution.
In the above example, STATE is changed to "PA".
If you enter too many words, it is an error and your CLIST is not executed.

Brief comparison with REXX ARG.
REXX has the ARG statement which also can pick up data entered on the command line when a REXX program is executed.
Assume this REXX ARG statement.
ARG NAME ADDR PHONE.
Assume that the above ARG is in a REXX program named TESTPRC1, and that it is executed like this on the command line of TSO/ISPF Option 6:
==> TESTPRC1 **john 148a 2125554583**

Upon execution, some of the REXX variables will be set.
> NAME will equal "JOHN"
> ADDR will equal "148A"
> PHONE will equal "2125554583"

Data is uppercased by the ARG statement. (But you can leave it as typed, if you change the ARG to PARSE ARG.)
All the variables specified on the ARG statement are set to something. But you don't have to enter anything. In that case, all are set to null (zero characters.)
You are entering words, and there cannot be spaces in a word. Putting values in quotes doesn't work.
If you enter only 1 word, the first variable NAME is set and the others are set to null. If you enter 2, the first two variables are set and the others are set to null. Same for 3.
There is no prompting with REXX, if you don't enter one or more of the values for the variables on the ARG statement.
If you enter too many words, the excess words are contained in the last variable, along with the expected information.

Continued on the next left-hand page.

REXX program continued from previous right-hand page.

```
PARM_WAS_ENTERED_OR_ASK:
"CLS" /* CLEAR THE SCREEN. DELETE IF YOU DON'T HAVE THIS PROGRAM */
DO I = 1 TO NUM_POS_PARMS
   IF DEBUG = "YES" THEN SAY POS_ENTERED.I "IS THE ARG FOR " I
   IF DEBUG = "YES" THEN SAY SYMBOL("POS_ENTERED.I") "SYMBOL"
   /* "OR" CHARACTER, ON NEXT LINE, IS HEX 4F */
   IF POS_ENTERED.I = "" | SYMBOL("POS_ENTERED.I") = "LIT"
       THEN CALL GET_POS_PARM POS_PARM.I I
       ELSE INTERPRET POS_PARM.I " = POS_ENTERED.I"
END I
RETURN


GET_POS_PARM:
SAY "ENTER POSITIONAL PARAMETER" POS_PARM.I
PULL ENTRY
IF ENTRY = "" THEN SIGNAL NO_POS_PARM_ENTERED
INTERPRET POS_PARM.I "= ENTRY"
IF DEBUG = "YES" THEN SAY VALUE(POS_PARM.I)
RETURN


VERIFY_INPUT:
/* CHECK FOR "(" AMONG POSITIONALS */
DO J = 1 TO NUM_POS_PARMS
   TEMP = POS_ENTERED.J
   IF POS("(",TEMP) > 0 THEN DO
       SAY "POSITIONAL PARAMETER" POS_ENTERED.J "CONTAINS PAREN"
       SAY "ONLY KEYWORD PARAMETERS CAN CONTAIN PARENS. TERMINATING"
       EXIT
       END
END J

/* CHECK FOR TOO MANY PARAMETERS, IN ALL */
IF WORDS(CMD_LINE_ENTERED) > (NUM_POS_PARMS + NUM_KEY_PARMS)
   THEN DO
       SAY "TOO MANY PARAMETERS ENTERED ON COMMAND LINE"
       SAY "MAX IS " NUM_POS_PARMS "POSITIONAL "
       SAY "AND    " NUM_KEY_PARMS "KEYWORD. TERMINATING"
       EXIT
       END
```

REXX program Continued on next right-hand page.

Supplement 3: REXX Program that Mimics CLIST PROC

Continued from previous left-hand page

Other differences in action.

When executing a CLIST, commas on the command line are ignored. They do nothing. They are treated exactly like spaces.

When executing REXX, commas on the command line cause trouble. Do not separate the values with commas. Commas do not have any special meaning on the command line. Separate the parameters with spaces.

Initial CLIST PROC must be the first executable statement in the program. Blank lines and comment lines don't count.

Initial REXX ARG can be anywhere in the program (but not in a subroutine or a function). I always put the initial ARG first.

REXX program continued from previous right-hand page.

```
/*  CHECK EVERY WORD ON CMD LINE CONTAINING "(" */
TEMP_CONCAT = ""
/* STRING ALL VALID KEYWORDS TOGETHER INTO ONE VARIABLE */
DO P2 = 1 TO NUM_KEY_PARMS
    TEMP_CONCAT = TEMP_CONCAT KEY_PARM.P2
END P2

DO P = 1 TO WORDS(CMD_LINE_ENTERED)

    TEMP = WORD(CMD_LINE_ENTERED, P)
    IF POS("(", TEMP) = 0 THEN ITERATE /* IGNORE IF NO ( */

    PARSE VAR TEMP TEMP "("      /* DROP "(" AND WHAT FOLLOWS */
    TEMP = TEMP"("               /* PUT BACK THE "(" */

    IF POS(TEMP, TEMP_CONCAT) = 0 THEN DO
       SAY "KEYWORD ENTERED " TEMP " IS NOT DEFINED"
       SAY "TERMINATING"
       EXIT
       END
END P

/* CHECK FOR BALANCED PARENS */
CTR_LEFT_PARENS  = 0
CTR_RIGHT_PARENS = 0
DO Q = 1 TO LENGTH(CMD_LINE_ENTERED)
    IF SUBSTR(CMD_LINE_ENTERED, Q, 1) = "("
       THEN CTR_LEFT_PARENS  = CTR_LEFT_PARENS + 1
    IF SUBSTR(CMD_LINE_ENTERED, Q, 1) = ")"
       THEN CTR_RIGHT_PARENS = CTR_RIGHT_PARENS + 1
END Q
IF CTR_LEFT_PARENS <> CTR_RIGHT_PARENS
THEN DO
     SAY "UNBALANCED PARENTHESES ON INPUT. TERMINATING"
     EXIT
     END
IF POS("((", CMD_LINE_ENTERED) > 0 THEN DO
     SAY "UNBALANCED PARENTHESES ON INPUT. TERMINATING"
     EXIT
     END
IF POS("))", CMD_LINE_ENTERED) > 0 THEN DO
     SAY "UNBALANCED PARENTHESES ON INPUT. TERMINATING"
     EXIT
     END
RETURN /* FOR VERIFY_INPUT */
```

REXX program Continued on next right-hand page.

Supplement 3: REXX Program that Mimics CLIST PROC

This page intentionally left blank

REXX program continued from previous right-hand page.

```
DISPLAY_INPUT:
SAY "POSITIONAL PARAMETERS AS RESOLVED"
DO K = 1 TO NUM_POS_PARMS
    SAY POS_PARM.K VALUE(POS_PARM.K)
END K
RETURN


PROCESS_KEYWORDS:
DO M = 1 TO KEY_PARM.0
    PARSE UPPER VAR KEY_PARM.M KW "(" KW_VALUE ")"
    INTERPRET KW "= KW_VALUE"  /* SET DEFAULT VALUE */
    KW2   = SPACE(KW"(",0)       /* ADD PAREN, DROP SPACES, IF ANY */
    IF POS(KW2, CMD_LINE_ENTERED) > 0
        THEN DO
             PARSE UPPER VAR CMD_LINE_ENTERED (KW2) KW3 ")"
             INTERPRET    KW "= KW3"
             END
END M
RETURN


DISPLAY_INPUT_KEYWORDS:
SAY "KEYWORD    PARAMETERS AS RESOLVED"
DO N = 1 TO KEY_PARM.0
 /*SAY KEY_PARM.N     */
    PARSE UPPER VAR KEY_PARM.N KW "("
    INTERPRET "SAY KW "  KW
/*   SAY "THIS";SAY KW     VALUE(KW)   */
/* SAY          KEY_PARM.N VALUE(KEY_PARM.N)   */
END N
RETURN


NO_POS_PARM_ENTERED:
SAY "YOU DID NOT ENTER A REQUIRED POSITIONAL PARAMETER. TERMINATING"
EXIT
```

This page intentionally left blank

Supplement 4: Programs that Use DBCS Data

Both CLIST and REXX can handle Double Byte Character Set (DBCS) data. There are only a few functions in CLIST that correspond to functions in REXX. These two sample programs will illustrate basic manipulation of DBCS in both languages.

Supplement 4 contains:
      CLIST
      REXX Program

Supplement 4: Programs that Use DBCS Data

CLIST

This program shows two ways of creating DBCS data in a CLIST. It illustrates the CLIST functions &SYSCSUBSTR, &SYSCLENGTH, &SYSONEBYTE, and &SYSTWOBYTE.

First, you need to delimit the DBCS string with HEX '0E' and HEX '0F'. To enter these non-printable, hex strings in the ISPF editor, do as follows:

On command line, type HEX:
```
EDIT         userid.TEST1.CLIST(CLST0061) - 01.01          Columns 00001 00072
Command ===>    HEX                                        Scroll ===> CSR
000008 SET DBCS_STRING =   " D1F2D3 "
```

Result:
```
EDIT         userid.TEST1.CLIST(CLST0061) - 01.01          Columns 00001 00072
Command ===>                                               Scroll ===> CSR
000008 SET DBCS_STRING =   " D1F2D3 "
       ECE4CCCE6EEDCDC474470CFCFCF07444444444444
       25304232D2399570E00FE416243FF000000000000
```

Type 0E, vertically, after the first quote; also 0F, verticaly, before the last quote.
```
EDIT         userid.TEST1.CLIST(CLST0061) - 01.01          Columns 00001 00072
Command ===>                                               Scroll ===> CSR
000008 SET DBCS_STRING =   " D1F2D3 "
       ECE4CCCE6EEDCDC474470CFCFCF07444444444444
       25304232D2399570E00FE416243FF000000000000
```

Type **HEX OFF** on the command line.

The CLIST continues on the next right-hand page.

Supplement 4: Programs that Use DBCS Data

You enter non-printable hex strings into a REXX program exactly as you do for a CLIST, as shown on the facing page.

```
/* CLST0061 TO ILLUSTRATE DBCS DATA */

/* SETTING A STRING TO DBCS  */
/* THE CHARACTER AFTER OPEN   QUOTE IS HEX 'OE'  */
/* THE CHARACTER BEFORE CLOSE QUOTE IS HEX 'OF'  */
SET DBCS_STRING = &STR( D1F2D3 )

WRITE CHECKING IF DBCS_STRING IS ACTUALLY DBCS:
WRITE &DATATYPE(&DBCS_STRING)
WRITE

WRITE TRYING THE SYSCSUBSTR FUNCTION ON DBCS_STRING
WRITE &SYSCSUBSTR(2:3,&DBCS_STRING) /* GIVES ":F2D3:" */
WRITE


WRITE TRYING THE SYSCLENGTH FUNCTION ON DBCS_STRING
WRITE &SYSCLENGTH(&DBCS_STRING) /* GIVES 3    */
WRITE

WRITE CONVERTING BACK TO ONE BYTE WITH SYSONEBYTE  (DOESN'T WORK)
SET ONE_BYTE_STRING = &SYSONEBYTE(&DBCS_STRING)
WRITE &ONE_BYTE_STRING
WRITE &DATATYPE(&ONE_BYTE_STRING)
WRITE

WRITE ANOTHER WAY TO CREATE A DBCS STRING WITH SYSTWOBYTE
SET DBCS_STRING2 = &SYSTWOBYTE(ABCD)
WRITE &DATATYPE(&DBCS_STRING2)
WRITE
```

REXX

This program shows two ways of creating a DBCS character string. It illustrates the REXX functions DBTODBCS, DBTOSBCS, LENGTH and SUBSTR.

```
/* REXX REXX0061 TO TEST DBCS FUNCTIONS */
OPTIONS "EXMODE"     /* REQUIRED BEFORE YOU CAN USE DBCS DATA */
                     /* ACCORDING TO THE MANUAL                */
SAY "SETTING A VARIABLE TO DBCS"
/* THE CHARACTER AFTER QUOTE        IS HEX 'OE'  */
/* THE CHARACTER AFTER QUOTE        IS HEX 'OF'  */
DBCS_STRING =  " D1F2D3 "
SAY DBCS_STRING
SAY DATATYPE(DBCS_STRING,D)          "         1 MEANS DBCS"


SAY "CONVERTING CHARACTER STRING TO DBCS WITH DBTODBCS FUNCTION"
DBCS_STRING2 = DBTODBCS("ABCD")
SAY DATATYPE(DBCS_STRING2,D)         "         1 MEANS DBCS"


 SAY "CONVERTING BACK TO SINGLE BYTE WITH DBTOSBCS FUNCTION"
 SINGLE_BYTE  = DBTOSBCS(DBCS_STRING2)
 SAY SINGLE_BYTE

 SAY "TRYING THE DBWIDTH FUNCTION"
 SAY DBWIDTH(DBCS_STRING)     "DBWIDTH OF DBCS_STRING "
 SAY DBWIDTH(DBCS_STRING2)    "DBWIDTH OF DBCS_STRING2"

 SAY "TRYING THE LENGTH FUNCTION ON DBCS DATA"
 SAY LENGTH(DBCS_STRING)

 SAY "TRYING THE SUBSTR FUNCTION ON DBCS DATA"
 SAY SUBSTR(DBCS_STRING,2,1)
```

This page intentionally left blank

Index

Index

Index

Index

Index

Index

Index

Index

Index

Index

Index

Index

By the same author

The REXX Language on TSO
ISBN-10: 1479104779, ISBN-13: 978-1479104772   (Published September 5, 2012)
How to use REXX to program on z/OS TSO/ISPF.

The REXX Language on TSO: REXX Functions   (Published July 13, 2013)
ISBN-10: 1490536078, ISBN-13: 978-1490536071
The built-in functions that are an integral part of the REXX language.

TSO CLIST to TSO REXX: Conversion Handbook
ISBN-10: 1508668493, ISBN-13: 978-1508668497   (Published May 1, 2015)
If you are converting CLIST programs to REXX, you will find this book useful.

Legacy Languages: Model COBOL programs with logic examples.
ISBN-13: 979-8694086097
(Published Oct 29, 2020)
Actual programs you can use as a model to create programs to solve common business programming problems.

Italian Dialogues: Learn Italian by Speaking Italian
ISBN-13: 979-8607849764   (Published August 10, 2020)

Italian Pronunciation
ISBN-13: 978-1976097997
ISBN-10: 1976097991   (Published June 27, 2018)

ESL: 17 Student Questions Answered
Clear answers to questions posed by students in ESL class.
ISBN-13: 978-1721980390
ISBN-10: 1721980393   (Published July 27, 2018)

French Expressions
Popular French expressions explained.
ISBN-13: 978-1489573476
ISBN-10: 148957347X   (Published June 9, 2013)
Kindle Edition: ASIN: B008UDGCZ6

Idiotismes, locutions, et expressions américains
Popular American expressions explained, and translated into French.
(French Edition)
By Gabriel F. Gargiulo
ISBN-13: 978-1490495583 ISBN-10: 1490495584   (Published June 29, 2013)
Kindle Edition: ASIN: B008PX0SWO   (Published July 26, 2012)